This book is about on  family who supported him, the people he nurtured, ... company he helped build. In *Where the Rubber Meets the Road*, we are reminded that humility, a warm smile, and a ready word of encouragement are always appropriate. Paul Zurcher's legacy calls us to remember that the future belongs to those who keep on learning, and that taking time for family and running a major business are not mutually exclusive priorities. He had figured out long before the textbook writers that honoring people and building healthy relationships, when coupled with the energy that comes from a vision undergirded by unquestioned personal integrity, are keys to building a vibrant and sustainable business. This story is truly remarkable. I highly recommend it.

Dr. Gene Habecker
President, Taylor University (2005-2016)

Paul Zurcher, as the author says, "lived a life of integrity and intentionality," and that life is captured powerfully in this book. I knew Paul to be a generous, caring, and faithful man, so I am delighted to endorse this book. It would be a great Sunday school class study, a mentoring guide for a men's group, or just a personal growth book for any individual. Full of heart-warming stories and a valuable set of principles that shaped Paul's life, the book provides lessons, inspiration, and practical wisdom that will bless any reader.

Michael J. Coyner
Retired United Methodist Bishop

Paul's philosophy in life was to listen and understand before making decisions. His emotional side was rooted in respect, no matter what the situation or the people involved. Paul used his faith to guide his principles and his heart to communicate what he believed in.

John Gamauf
Retired President, Consumer Tires,
Bridgestone Firestone North American Tire

We are inspired as we read and reflect on the life of Paul Zurcher. Inspired that we, mostly ordinary people, can—with courage, optimism, hard work, and faith—accomplish great things. As we reflect, we observe that these things can be accomplished, not at the expense of others, but while assisting them to aspire and to grow as well. This record of a life defines leadership beyond hollow success into discipleship in the Christian sense.

Dr. Jay Kesler
President Emeritus, Taylor University

"I serve God by selling tires." These words define the life of one of the most incredible men to ever live on planet Earth. Paul Zurcher was a true American hero. Growing up in a small rural farming community in Indiana, he then went on to serve our great nation in the second World War (where he escaped life-threatening injuries from a bullet just inches from his heart), and later to build one of our country's most successful business enterprises. Paul impacted thousands of people over the course of his life, and he built his life, his family, and his business on nine principles which defined the way he lived, led, and worked.

Our world needs more leaders like Paul Zurcher. There are very few like him. Read his story, learn from his principles, and you will be blessed, encouraged, and strengthened. I encourage you to learn from Paul's life and his nine principles. I hope you will find and define your own life's purpose and develop your own principles for living so that you can impact thousands of lives as well.

Ray Hilbert
Co-Founder, Truth at Work
International Best-Selling Author

Where
the Rubber
Meets
the Road

Nine Proven Principles
from the Life
of Paul Zurcher

**by Melinda Zurcher
with Rachel Starr Thomson**

Where the Rubber Meets the Road: Nine Proven Principles from the Life of Paul Zurcher
Copyright ©2017 Melinda Zurcher with Rachel Starr Thomson

Published by
Deep River Books
Sisters, Oregon
www.deepriverbooks.com

ISBN-13: 9781632694461
Library of Congress: 2017941662

Printed in the United States of America.

Cover Design by Joe Bailen, Contajus Designs

DEDICATION

To the Zurcher Family—

Paul and Betty's children: Larry, Mark, and Colleen

Grandchildren: Lindsey, Tina, Jon, Brittney, Jackie, and Maureen

Great-grandchildren: Kale, Hailey, Daniel, Kley, Larissa, Bria, Asher, McKenna, Gwen, and Sonja

Thank you for entrusting me with Grandpa's story. Much love!

TIMELINE OF PAUL'S LIFE

July 9, 1924	Paul's birth
1945	Drafted, trained at Camp Hood, and sent to fight in Italy
April 19, 1945	Shot in shoulder during the Battle of Po Valley
1948	Opened Zurcher Tire in Monroe, Indiana
July 16, 1949	Married Betty Schug
June 26, 1952	Birth of son—Larry
November 24, 1954	Birth of son—Mark
November 2, 1956	Birth of daughter—Colleen
1964	Partnered with Jim Wertenberger in Wertenberger Tire (Huntington, IN)
1965	Became a partner in Bluffton Tire (Bluffton, IN)
1966	Partnered with Ray Monteith in Monteith Tire (Warsaw, IN)
1969	Expanded into Fort Wayne with McMahon Tire (Ft. Wayne, IN)
1971	Partnered with Paul Weaver and Ray Monteith in Southern Indiana Tire, Inc. (Princeton, IN)

1974	Joined Paul Swentzel and Don Schneider in S&S Firestone, Inc. (Lexington, KY)
1977	Partnered with Ken Langhals in K&M Tire, Inc. (Delphos, OH)
1989–1999	Served on Taylor University Board of Trustees
1998	Stores adopted Best-One brand name
1999	Inducted into the Tire Industry Association Hall of Fame
2005	Partner in over 250 Best-One locations
2005	Received award for selling over 50 million Bridgestone Firestone tires
2005	Awarded Modern Tire Dealer of the Year
2008	Received honorary doctorate from Taylor University
2014	Presented with Sagamore of the Wabash Award from the governor of Indiana
May 7, 2015	Paul's death
April 3, 2016	Betty's death

CONTENTS

PREFACE

This is the book everyone told Paul Zurcher he needed to write. In response, he would always chuckle, and with a twinkle in his eye, respond that was something he would do when he started to slow down. Anyone who knew Paul realized he was highly unlikely to slow down anytime soon. Paul died at the age of ninety still "living life wide open," as he liked to say. He still worked six days a week, drove to business meetings around the Midwest, visited his wife with Alzheimer's, and spoke at church and community events.

As Paul's granddaughter-in-law, I was persistent in encouraging him to write a book because I believed people, including myself, could benefit from his wisdom and life lessons. One of my life regrets is that we did not write this book together, but I know Grandpa would say God had a greater plan.

Paul was an avid reader, so I do believe he would be honored by the idea of creating a book. Paul often quoted one of his favorite authors, Charlie "Tremendous" Jones, who said, "You will be the same in five years as you are today except for the people you meet and the books you read."[1] When Paul first read this in his early twenties, he committed to reading an average of an hour and a half every day and kept to that commitment until the day he died. In this same spirit, my prayer is that this book will not leave readers the same as they are today but encourage them to live the lives God intended for them.

This collection of stories and quotes stems from many of Paul's speeches and personal notes, as well as my interviews with family and friends. Paul lived a powerful life characterized by integrity and intentionality. Accordingly, this book has been arranged around the framework of his "Nine Life Principles." Paul gradually developed these principles based on his experiences and lived them out faithfully; they seemed an appropriate grid through which to tell his story. Our prayer as the Zurcher family is that these glimpses into our father and grandfather's life, thoughts, and prayers will continue to point others toward Christ even though Paul is gone from this earth. I know exactly what Paul would say if that happened—his favorite word: Fantastic!

Mindy Zurcher,
On behalf of Paul's three children,
Larry, Mark, and Colleen, and the
extended Zurcher family

INTRODUCTION

Inside an abandoned barn nestled in the Italian Alps, the air was surprisingly peaceful. Snowflakes of dust danced in the sunlight and landed on stacks of feed for long-forgotten livestock. Three young men in combat field uniforms crouched in the hazy stillness, letting their eyes adjust to the gloom as their hearts pounded from their dash down the hill. Their weapons rested in their hands.

Outside, the crackle of machine-gun fire and the rhythmic pounding of mortar told them it wasn't over.

The year was 1945, and the war was not going well for the Axis powers. The Americans and Allies advanced throughout Europe; the tide of the war had turned. But for the boys in the barn, young men barely out of high school who had just watched many of their friends gunned down by Germans on the village rooftops, turning tides made little difference. Here and now, bullets killed.

A sudden explosion threw all three soldiers to the ground. A mortar shell had landed just behind the barn. Another shell whistled through the air and exploded in front of them. Without saying a word, the soldiers knew the enemy was honing in on their target, and the next shell would land directly on top of them.

* * *

What seemed like only minutes before, these young men had advanced on the village at the bottom of Po Valley. One of them, twenty-year-old Paul Zurcher, dove into the nearest ditch and pressed his body into the ground, letting a foot of water and mud seep over him. Eleven weeks of boot camp had never prepared him for this. He had intended to be part of the artillery when he was drafted, but the casualties at the front were so heavy that basic training was cut short and hundreds of soldiers, Paul included, were shipped out to replace them. He had become part of a machine-gun squad, helping to bring up ammunition and load the guns.

Bullets riddled the hillside even as the sergeant called, "Advance! Over the top, boys!" The first wave of Americans swept down into the village, but the Germans were ready for them with machine guns in second-story windows and on top of roofs. Their guns trained on any soldiers cresting the ridge.

In the shelter of the rocks and ditch, Paul took a moment to catch his breath and felt for the reassurance of the Bible tucked in his chest pocket. The pages were not even wet, he had pressed his body so tightly against the ground. He whispered one last prayer, "Lord, help us," and sprang up and over the embankment.

* * *

That charge had carried some of them through the deadly streets into the barn. Now, with a grim nod to one another, the three young soldiers lined up at the barn door with weapons ready. On the count of three, the first soldier ran out the door and was immediately filled with bullets—shot over forty times by a German machine gun. The second soldier followed close behind and was gunned down as well.

Still fearing a mortar shell, Paul jumped from the shelter of the doorway, looking for an escape route. A blinding pain tore through his shoulder. He looked down. Blood seeped through his uniform. He ducked back into the cover of the barn and slumped against the wall.

His adrenaline continued pumping as he tried to stanch the flow of blood and reload his pistol. He expected at any moment the Germans would hit the barn with a shell or enter and take him prisoner.

But as the minutes lengthened, the gunfire seemed to lighten and move farther down the hill. Paul peeked through a crack between the wall planks. His fallen friends lay crumpled in the dust of the farmyard; there was no sign of enemy soldiers.

Paul waited in the barn for hours until darkness cloaked the mountains. He ripped off part of his uniform and tied the fabric as best he could over his wound. Then he eased out the barn door and ran away from the battle zone.

A bullet ricocheted past his ear as he ran, and Paul zigzagged up the hillside despite the pain radiating from his shoulder. He could just make out in the distance a house with a light in the window and a Red Cross flag draped over the door. With the last of his strength, Paul sprinted across the yard and collapsed through the doorway.

Lying on the floor, Paul looked up into the faces of an army nurse and two other soldiers. The nurse brushed the hair from his eyes. "There now, Soldier. You're going to be all right."

Paul let out a deep breath that he seemed to have been holding for hours. He could still see his friends lying in the dust and taste the bitter tang of fear and grief. Was he safe? Had he really made it? Why him, and not the others?

Lord, help us.

The two soldiers lifted Paul onto the bed, and the nurse went about examining his bullet wound and cleaning it as best she could. "The only medicine we have is penicillin," she said apologetically, "so that will have to get you through until we can transfer you to the hospital in Florence."

Paul nodded and laid his head back on the pillow. Despite the pain, he was overcome with weariness and fell asleep to the rhythm of machine guns firing in the distance.

* * *

World War II was a life-defining part of Paul Zurcher's story—but like so many in his generation, he never told it. Not until almost seventy years later, in conversation with his granddaughter Maureen, did Paul begin to share details from his war days—details that went beyond the iconic story of the barn to the losses and horrors he had witnessed. His hands shook as he talked. "I've never told anyone," he said. "I've never talked about this."

In one of those twists of irony we can only attribute to the hand of God, the close call in the barn that day likely saved Paul's life. He was sent home to recover. After a few months' leave, while driving to a train station in Indianapolis to be shipped to the Pacific Theater, V-J Day was declared.

The war was over, and Paul Zurcher's life had been given back to him—to make of it whatever he would.

At age ninety, Paul was supposed to take part in an honor flight for World War II vets in Fort Wayne, Indiana. Maureen had talked him into it. He and other vets from the cornfields of Indiana would be flown in a chartered plane to the National World War II Memorial in Washington, DC, for the day, then return home to be greeted with fanfare and recognition by their community.

Initially, Paul was told a wheelchair would be made available for him. He wanted nothing to do with *that*—he could walk on his own, thank you very much. But illness struck shortly before the ceremony, an infection that led to the discovery of cancer. He could ignore it, the doctors said, and it would likely kill him. But then, he was ninety. How much longer did he have left to live? Or he could risk surgery.

Paul chose the risk. His wife, stricken with advanced Alzheimer's, needed him to stick around for a few more years. Not only that, he still worked in his business every day. He couldn't quit now.

But, well, he would need that wheelchair for the ceremony after all.

Paul came through the surgery, but the doctor had warned about the recovery. The stress turned out to be too hard on Paul's heart. Two weeks after the surgery, on May 7, 2015, Paul Zurcher passed from this world.

To his family, Paul's death came as a shock. Yes, he was ninety—but he was *alive*. He was a man who didn't plan to die; he planned to live. Over and over again at the funeral others agreed they could never really fathom Paul dying. Rick Hursell, the manager of Best-One Tire of Angola, reflected, "We were never ready to say goodbye. We thought Paul would live forever, you know. At his age and his health, we would jokingly say, 'We'd like to know your secret to life.'"

The young man whose life was saved by a bullet just inches from his heart had made something truly remarkable of his life. Maybe it was the perspective given him in that barn that caused him to embrace life the way he did. Maybe it was the principles taught in that Bible in his pocket, or even more, the God who had written them. After all, many people come through traumatic events broken and destroyed. Paul came through revitalized, full of character and integrity, full of passion for life, people, and God.

And he didn't keep it to himself. Jeff Kirk, a longtime employee of Zurcher's Best-One Tire & Service, the organization Paul founded and built to become one of the largest independent tire distributors in the United States, shared in a voice trembling with warmth, "None of us are the same as we were when we started here. Paul helped us all find our way."

To many who knew him, Paul Zurcher was the embodiment of the Greatest Generation: a man of courage, integrity, enthusiasm, and faith. His life wasn't easy. But it was a *gift*.

That perspective empowered everything he did.

* * *

Paul Zurcher was born July 9, 1924, to a Quaker farming family near Monroe, Indiana. Surrounded by cornfields and Amish communities, the Zurchers were down-to-earth people to whom family, faith, and hard work were paramount. Like most young men from farming backgrounds, Paul stayed in school only until the eighth grade and then went to work on the family farm.

Although pacifism was a historical tenet of Quakerism, World Wars I and II strained that commitment. Paul's older brother, Art, was sent to fight in North Africa in WWII. Paul actually ran into Art on a delay, but the two brothers initially did not recognize each other, so changed were they by the war.

At nineteen, Paul had a deferment to work on the family farm, but heavy casualties at the front necessitated more soldiers. Paul was drafted and sent to Camp Hood in Texas for an unusually short time of boot camp and then fought in Italy, where his near brush with death sent him home. "Only a few inches, from my shoulder to my heart, was the distance between my death and continued life," Paul would later point out.

When the war ended, Paul received a Purple Heart in honor of his heroic service and seventeen hundred dollars from the GI Bill. Paul said in an interview, "I gave back my uniform and only kept my gun, my Purple Heart, and the book written about my unit in the mountaineers." He preferred to forget the atrocities of war and begin his life anew.

Paul used the money from the GI Bill to buy a torpedo-shaped, robin's-egg-blue Oldsmobile Chevrolet that he hoped would attract the attention of a special young lady. It worked! The car—or maybe something about Paul himself—was impressive enough to attract the attention of Betty Schug; the couple married in 1949. The marriage caused quite a stir in the community, as Betty was exceedingly beautiful and "a catch," yet Paul whisked her off her feet. He was twenty-five, and she was nineteen. Together they grew to a family of five, as Larry, Mark, and Colleen were later added.

Nothing about those earlier years pointed to the remarkable future ahead. Paul hadn't come back from the war with grandiose plans of personal advancement, just with a zeal for life and commitment to serve God and others. His father hoped he would come back to the farm, and his mother wanted him to be a banker, but Paul took a job at a local service station in Monroe.

While he pumped gas one day, an older friend who recognized Paul's potential challenged him to do more with his life. He said, "You know, Paul, I've been watching you for six months, and I've never seen such a waste." Startled, Paul asked what he meant.

The friend said, "Paul, there is no doubt in my mind that if you went into business for yourself, worked really hard, and started believing in yourself, you could go all the way to the top."

With that prompt, Paul got a three-hundred-dollar loan from the First Bank of Berne and bought a closed fueling station in his hometown. Paul Zurcher was in business. His fueling and auto shop had only one bay, so much of the initial work on vehicles had to be done outdoors despite Indiana's frigid winters and sweltering summers.

The rest is history. After several years in the business, Paul came to focus on distributing and servicing tires. Through partnerships and gradually opening more stores, Paul's tire business expanded to over 280 stores throughout twenty-five states, with retail, commercial, wholesale, and retread locations. In 1998, all the stores came under the common banner of Best-One Tire. His unique business model featured partnerships with others, rather than consolidating his ownership.

"Paul never gave anything but an opportunity," Jeff Kirk said. "It was up to you to take it or not."

Paul's Nine Life Principles

When Paul was a young man, he noticeably stuttered. One newcomer to the Berne area remembers hearing him speak and wondering if the organization hosting him couldn't have found someone better. However, she retracted her opinion after hearing the depth of Paul's message.

As in other areas of his life, Paul committed to improving his public speaking and became a powerful motivational speaker. He spoke to churches, schools, Rotary Clubs, business professionals, charitable organizations, and fellow veterans. When Paul passed away, he left behind a binder of his printed speeches almost four inches thick. He also missed two more speaking engagements scheduled at a university and a church.

One speech in particular best summarizes Paul's wisdom and life lessons. In it, Paul shared about his nine life commitments, one of his favorite topics. About these principles, Paul wrote, "They didn't come to me all at once, but rather, the list has been developed and built upon for the past fifty years. I live by all nine on a daily basis."

When Paul began speaking at schools and community events, he printed these commitments on business cards to hand out to others. When asked about them, Paul quoted Rick Warren.

> Nothing shapes your life more than the commitments you choose to make. Your commitments can develop you or they can destroy you, but either way, they will define you. Tell me what you are committed to, and I'll tell you what you will be in twenty years. We become whatever we are committed to.[1]

These are Paul's Nine Life Principles:

1. To seek God's friendship, fellowship, and guidance
2. To develop effective relationships
3. To treat everyone with honor, love, dignity, and respect
4. To be self-disciplined and self-controlled
5. To do the right things right
6. To be a positive, enthusiastic, and passionate person
7. To never compromise my integrity
8. To plan for tomorrow today
9. To live life now, and live it wide open

Paul's Nine Life Principles provide the structure for this book. Each chapter begins with a life principle and Paul's description of the principle from one of his speeches. He stood in front of many a crowd, always smiling broadly and with a twinkle in his eye, delivering these very words. When reading Paul Zurcher's own words, his fervency and love for others jump off the page.

> *There is nothing quite as potent as a focused life, one lived on purpose.*
> — *Rick Warren*

Following Paul's explanation of each commitment are stories from his life that illustrate how he lived out what he believed. What made Paul's life distinct from so many others was the way his words and life aligned. This speaks to his sincerity and commitment—and at the same time, points to the potential we all possess.

As Paul quoted from Rick Warren, "There is nothing quite as potent as a focused life, one lived on purpose."[2]

Our hope in writing this book is that you too will see your life as a gift and will give it the focus, purpose, and commitment needed to live it to the fullest.

PAUL ZURCHER'S NINE LIFE PRINCIPLES

1. To seek God's friendship, fellowship, and guidance
2. To develop effective relationships
3. To treat everyone with honor, love, dignity, and respect
4. To be self-disciplined and self-controlled
5. To do the right things right
6. To be a positive, enthusiastic, and passionate person
7. To never compromise my integrity
8. To plan for tomorrow today
9. To live life now, and live it wide open

PRINCIPLE #1

To Seek God's Friendship, Fellowship, and Guidance

This commitment is actually twofold: opening yourself to God's guidance, and asking him for the power to do what he asks of you.

What is the best way to develop your relationship with God? Through prayer. It says in Luke 11:9–10, "Ask and it will be given to you; seek and you will find; knock and the door will be opened to you. For everyone who asks receives; the one who seeks finds; and to the one who knocks, the door will be opened."

The heart of prayer is communion with God, and that communion is available anytime. He is always there like a treasured friend. The goal of prayer is friendship with God, living his life in the world. It's allowing yourself to trust in him, listening quietly for his guidance, and then asking him for the strength to do his will. Our God is not just all-powerful; he is power-sharing. He gives you the power to do whatever he asks of you. God wants you to tap into his power—all you have to do is ask. The power that comes from prayer is available to all of us.

I'd like to tell you a story about the simple faith this commitment describes. One night a little girl surprised her mother when she ended her prayer by saying, "And now, God, what can I do for you?" Like this little girl, we must condition our lives to be open to what God wants us to do for him. When we do that, we will see and serve God more clearly, love God more dearly, and follow God more nearly. We will be able to live life successfully by doing his will for us.

— Paul Zurcher, from his 2010 speech,
"Nine Life Commitments"

CHAPTER 1

*"The only way we can play a significant role in the
kingdom of God is to allow Jesus to live his life in and
through us. While apart from him we can do nothing, in
him we can do anything he calls us to do."*

— *Paul Zurcher*

"Paul, come on in now." Eva Zurcher's voice carried across the
barren Indiana cornfields. She sounded tired—tired from the
challenges of raising seven small children, tired of scratching out
a life on a tenant farm.

In response to his mother's call, Paul leapt across the muddy
creek and took off in a sprint. The bullfrogs in the distance
called to him, but he knew his game would have to wait until
tomorrow. His parents, Quakers of Swiss descent, expected
prompt obedience, so he didn't dawdle as some nine-year-old
boys might.

When he jogged up the steps of their white clapboard
farmhouse, Paul realized at once that something was amiss.
All his siblings sat somber and silent around the kitchen table.
His mother gestured to him, and Paul squeezed in next to his
younger brother Vernon on the long wooden bench.

Paul's father, William, stood at the head of the table. With
his broad shoulders, high forehead, and piercing dark eyes, no
one questioned his leadership of this home. William cleared his
throat, and all seven little heads turned. "We need to talk to you

all. Your mother and I are sorry, but we won't have any extra money this year for Christmas presents. With the harvest being so bad, we are going to have to do without this year."

Paul watched his siblings' faces work to mask their disappointment. They knew better than to protest or complain. Ever since the Depression started, money had been scarce, and they all worked hard on the farm just to eat.

With nothing to say to ease their disappointment, Eva turned to the stove to stir the beans and then passed out the cornbread. Paul squeezed Vernon's shoulder and whispered in his ear, "Tomorrow, we're going to figure out how to earn some money." Vernon gave a stiff nod, and Paul spent the rest of the meal mulling over ideas to buy those Christmas presents.

The next morning Paul slipped out of bed while the rest of the house slept, and gently roused Vernon. They pulled on their overalls and stepped out onto the small front porch. "What are you fixing to do, Paul?" Vernon whispered.

"We've got to find a way to buy those presents. I think we should go ask next door and see if they'll let us glean their fields after they're done harvesting. Their corn came in a lot better than ours."

Vernon snorted. "But that will take forever."

"I figure if we go every morning after our chores and before school we can get enough grain to sell, and then we can buy something out of the Sears Catalog for the kids," Paul said.

Each morning for the next several weeks, Paul and Vernon scoured the neighbor's cornfield for dropped and forgotten kernels of corn. Each plink in the metal bucket spurred them on, but it seemed as if the bucket refused to be filled. They always had to begin their mile-and-a-half walk to the country schoolhouse long before they were finished.

Finally one day, Paul announced, "Let's take what we have into town and see what they'll give us for it."

An hour later, Paul and Vernon walked out of the granary with broad grins across their suntanned faces. Paul clutched in his hand one dollar and twenty-five cents. It would be enough—enough to make all his siblings' dreams come true. The boys ran home and rushed to open the Sears Catalog. There it was. Paul pointed to the picture: thirty-three toys for ninety-nine cents. They carefully counted out the pennies, nickels, and dimes and placed their order in an envelope. The boys caught each other's eye and gave a knowing smile.

But the bounty left the boys with a quandary: they still had twenty-six cents. How to spend it?

They agonized over the question. Extra spending money was rare, and the boys were wary of wasting the opportunity. At last, they decided to walk to the store and buy some candy for themselves.

As they were leaving the house, Paul called out, "We're going into town to buy some candy."

But before they could leave, Eva called after them, "I don't think so, boys."

Both Vernon and Paul turned back, and their mother joined them on the porch. Wisps of Eva's dark curly hair escaped her bun, and her round cheeks were flushed from working over the hot stove. She leaned against the doorjamb and looked both boys straight in the eye.

"You're going to drop that money in the collection plate on Sunday," she said. "You know that you can't out-give the Lord."

As young as he was, what nine-year-old Paul felt in that moment wasn't just mother-imposed guilt—it was conviction. Hard as he had worked, it was the Lord who had enabled him and Vernon to meet their goal. His mother was right.

The boys did as their mother said and put the extra money in the offering plate. For Paul at least, this wasn't just a one-time event. It was a decision to be a friend of God—one of the first in a lifetime of such decisions.

Over ten years later, fighting a war with a Bible in his pocket, Paul still knew that his life was a gift of God, that all good gifts come from God, and that life needed to be lived with generosity and in fellowship with God. Even at the end of his life, a nurse in the hospital caring for ninety-year-old Paul asked him what he did for a living.

"I serve God by selling tires," he said.

In one of his speeches, Paul reflected on his faith:

> The only way we can play a significant role in the kingdom of God is to allow Jesus to live his life in and through us. While apart from him we can do nothing, in him we can do anything he calls us to do. The greatest blessings we can receive are not material in nature. They are the blessings of his infinite love and care for us. He delights in showering us with good things—but we must present our requests to him. And once we know his will, we have a responsibility to embrace his direction and obey him completely.

Gleaning cornfields or selling tires, fighting a war or raising a family, Paul never lost that fellowship with God.

* * *

"When you knock on the door of God's heart through prayer and thanksgiving, he opens himself up to you."

— *Paul Zurcher*

More than sixty years after he dropped that twenty-six cents in the offering plate, Paul rested his head in his hands as he reflected on his reading, his fingers tracing over the Bible passage he'd just read. Seated at a small desk surrounded by open books, Paul began to scratch a few notes on a yellow legal pad. He took another book off the shelf, which overflowed with yet more books.

And so it went whenever Paul prepared his Sunday school lesson—something he did faithfully for over fifty years. Paul spent hours reading, praying, and preparing for his class each week, in addition to the hours he spent in personal study of the Scriptures for his own benefit. Oftentimes, Paul chose a word for the week and searched Scripture to find the meaning of the word to share with his class. One member of Paul's class, Brad Lehman, says, "Everyone would be fortunate if they had the opportunity to participate in Paul's class at least once. He had the ability to take a dry passage in Scripture and make it speak to you. He would find a Scripture and say, 'God would do that for me? He would do that for *me!* Wow! That's powerful.'"

As Paul continued to prepare his lesson, he'd sit and study at his small desk in the basement. Based on his surroundings, one would never suspect Paul was a successful business partner in hundreds of tire stores. The basement of his small ranch house had a low ceiling and burnt-orange carpet that hadn't been popular since the seventies. Other than the desk, the only furniture filling the room was a set of old lawn furniture. It was obvious Paul and Betty would rather make use of the old than throw out and buy new. A treadmill sat in the far corner, where Paul walked each morning while reading.

Betty once said, "I knew when I woke up in the morning where Paul would be. Down there walking and reading. He could stay down there for hours." Paul had a more dignified office on the main floor, but he took sanctuary in the basement where he could enjoy quiet time alone with God as well as a place to think through his day.

Paul knew a strong faith doesn't come easily. He once said,

> We are living in a day of instant formulas that sup-posedly can be applied to everything under the sun from TV dinners to "how to get rich in three easy lessons." Our push-button society and computerized age has conditioned us to think of presto-change-o solutions to a multitude of problems. We can flip a switch and have instant lights. We have instant pota-toes, one-minute rice, and even in Las Vegas there is a marquee in front of a chapel that reads, 'Instant Mar-riage, Everything Provided.' When it comes to spiri-tual growth and maturity, some Christians have fallen prey to this instantaneous type of thinking. We have a tendency to forget that at one time all of us were babes in Christ. I think most of us realize that there is no such thing as an instantly mature Christian. It takes time and effort to grow Christian maturity.

Rather than wanting it instantly, Paul put in the time and effort to grow his faith. He committed to saying a prayer each day written by Heartsill Wilson, who was at one time a popular Christian speaker. Paul's good friend and business partner, Ray Monteith, also prayed the same prayer, entitled "A New Day."

Paul intentionally chose how to begin each day. He was known to say that the most important eight minutes of the day were the first four minutes and the last four minutes. The first four minutes determined Paul's attitude for the day, and he

A New Day
This is the beginning of a new day.
God has given me this day to use as I will.
I can waste it—or use it for good,
but what I do today is important,
because I am exchanging a day of my life for it!
When tomorrow comes, this day will be gone forever,
leaving in its place something that I have traded for it.
I want it to be gain, and not loss;
good, and not evil;
success, and not failure;
in order that I shall not regret
the price that I have paid for it.[1]

committed the day to the Lord. During the last four minutes, as his head hit the pillow, Paul thanked God and reflected on what he had done for the Lord.

Paul not only began each day with prayer but continued praying throughout the day and asking God for guidance. Paul's grandson, Jon, remembers Paul calling for a break during a difficult business meeting filled with heated discussions. Rather than stretching his legs or grabbing a cup of coffee, Paul hung back and silently bowed his head in the empty conference room. Jon says, "I remember Grandpa closing his eyes and lowering his head. He didn't have to say a word, but I knew when he looked back up that he had been praying and asking for guidance on how to handle the situation."

When the other men came back into the room, there was a calm that hadn't been there a few minutes before. Paul opened the conversation in a different direction and was able to lead everyone toward an unexpected compromise. Stunned at the sudden turnaround, the other partners left the room chuckling and shaking their heads. They didn't understand how Paul always seemed to find a win-win solution to an impossible situation. But Paul knew the secret—the power of prayer.

"What is the greatest power in the universe?" Paul asked in a speech. "Is it the enormous force of the hurricane, or the tornado, or the tidal wave, or the earthquake, or the exploding volcano? These are indeed tremendous manifestations of nature's strength, but they are not the greatest power. What, then, is the greatest power in the universe? I believe that it is the mechanism by which man on earth establishes a connection that provides the flow of power between the mighty Creator and himself. And it is released and transmitted by means of a mechanism known as prayer."

Paul practiced those words. He often spent days before a meeting praying and thinking through solutions and his choice of words. Jon remembers, "Before meetings, Grandpa would spend a lot of time at home and in the car preparing and asking for the Lord's direction. I also remember several times when Grandpa and a partner would be trying to make a decision on something. They would be talking and then they would say, 'Well, let's just pray about this and seek the Lord's guidance to give us the right direction to go.'"

Really it was God, rather than Paul, who guided those meetings.

* * *

"Our strength lies in the Lord and not in ourselves. There is no comparison between the might and ability of God and of humankind. He is infinite; we are finite. When we rely on the Lord, we have access to his unlimited power and wisdom, and therefore, we will not end up as failures."

— *Paul Zurcher*

A comfortable silence hung over the family room. Paul lounged in a chair with a book open on his lap, and Betty sat on the couch watching a television program. Shifting in his chair, Paul cleared his throat and caught Betty's eye.

"A gentleman from Taylor University came to see me at the store today, and we went out to lunch."

Betty didn't respond but only nodded.

"He's the president there, and he wondered if I would like to be part of their board. He knows the Muselmans well; I think Art recommended me." Betty tried to keep a neutral face, but Paul could read her body language after forty years of marriage.

"Paul," she said, "you are already on too many committees. Between the stores, church, and meetings in Monroe, you hardly have a free night."

"I know I'm away a lot, and I don't like not being with you and the family. There's something different about this, though—I really feel like I should do it."

Betty let out a sigh and tucked her feet beneath her. "You should pray about it before you make any decision. Then you'll know what to do."

Despite Betty's hesitance, Paul did decide to join the board of trustees at Taylor University in Upland, Indiana. He served on the board for a number of years and helped lead one of the largest and most successful capital campaigns in the university's history. He believed God guided him to join the board for reasons of his own—and these reasons became clearer over the years.

Jay Kesler, who served as Taylor University's president for fifteen years, explained why he asked Paul to be part of his board. "Paul was a Taylor-type man. The word philosophers and theologians use to describe it is *irenic*, an 'irenic spirit.' That is, you have a spine, you have a backbone, but your spirit is open and gracious toward others. And Paul to me is kind of the personification of all that."

Even though Betty was initially hesitant about Paul joining the board, those at Taylor only felt her support. Jay said, "Paul was a big believer that we needed to invite our wives to the board meetings, let them see what was going on. Otherwise, the husband's going to be gone to a Taylor board meeting, and well, what does Taylor mean to her? It's just one more lonely night. If it's just one more lonely night, Taylor becomes the enemy. If she comes to Taylor and gets involved and hears the students' testimonies, then Taylor becomes part of her life too."

Jay remembers the way Betty and Paul honored and depended on each other. "Though Betty was a quiet lady, very quiet, she was definitely *there,* and Paul, when he made decisions, *looked* at her, and they communicated. He always wanted her affirming look. She might not have even smiled, but it was in her eyes. I learned to admire that very much in Paul. I knew that when I went to ask him for financial help for Taylor, he would want some time, and I knew during that time he would be talking to his wife." Betty and Paul together decided to continue serving and generously giving to Taylor for the coming decades.

The long-standing friendship between the university and Paul and Betty was honored in 2016 when Taylor named their new dining area Zurcher Commons, with plaques commemorating both of their lives. The plaques contain their biographies, Paul's favorite prayer from Heartsill Wilson, and his Nine Life Principles.

As is so often the case, Paul and Betty not only blessed Taylor with their service, but were blessed in return by the relationships they formed there.

The decision to join the Taylor board had other, more unexpected consequences. Paul liked to tell the story of how he once sat at a Taylor board meeting making small talk with another board member, Dr. Gentile. Paul asked him if there was one thing people should do to maintain good health. The doctor thought for a moment and then said, "Have a thorough physical each year at a large teaching hospital." Paul thanked him for the advice and said he would give it some thought.

Paul and Betty followed the doctor's recommendation and began to schedule yearly physicals at the Cleveland Clinic. They booked their appointments months in advance and stayed in a hotel room for the few days of tests and appointments. At one of these checkups, in 1994, the doctor returned with some somber news. Betty had a lump in her breast that looked serious. They wanted to do more tests to see if it was cancerous.

The tests confirmed the tumor was malignant, and the doctors quickly lined up Betty's surgery. She underwent a complete mastectomy followed by reconstructive surgery. The doctors marveled at how early the cancer had been found and applauded Paul and Betty for their preventative actions, which probably saved Betty's life.

These coincidences weren't lost on Paul. He realized that if God had not led him to the board at Taylor and Dr. Gentile had not recommended annual physicals, Betty's cancer might not have been found until it was too late. Paul often said that serving on the Taylor board saved his wife's life.

"We must become intimately connected with God and his purposes," Paul taught in his speech entitled, "Align Yourself with God's Will."

"When we are working in concert and harmony with God," he continued, "he's willing to give us the power to accomplish great things. We must be sure we're traveling the road he wants for us before we seek his help in moving down it. As we become more mature in our faith, we become more adept at discerning his will. We will learn to develop confidence that as we head in God's direction, we're going the right way—and he will become available to encourage and empower us."

The blessings from Taylor University continued to flow to Paul and Betty. In 2008, Paul was awarded an honorary doctorate for his lifetime of service and generosity. At the commencement, surrounded by his family and friends, Paul shared his Nine Life Principles with the graduating class. Even though he was elderly in the eyes of these undergraduates, the students sat in rapt attention as Paul shared a bit of his life story and the commitments that guided him.

This doctoral degree not only honored Paul's service but also his lifelong dedication to learning. He had completed only eight years of formal schooling yet continued to learn and read; his self-education surpassed others with formal degrees. Even in his eighties, he would point out discrepancies on a financial statement that no one else in the room noticed. The doctoral degree was well deserved, though Paul, in his humility, would probably disagree.

Paul's friendship with God led him to great successes in his business, personal life, and relationships. He knew the many gifts he enjoyed in life came direct from the Giver, whose fellowship he actively sought.

Questions to Ponder

Principle #1: To Seek God's Friendship, Fellowship, and Guidance

1. Paul's speech states, "This commitment is actually twofold: opening yourself to God's guidance and asking him for the power to do what he asks of you." Whatever your background may be, have you ever deliberately opened yourself to God and asked him for guidance and power? Have you considered that God may be asking you to do something? If your answer is no, why not? What might the results be in your life if you did?

2. Paul also said, "Our God is not just all-powerful; he is power-sharing." Is this a departure from how you have thought about God's power in the past? Have you considered that the power of God is accessible to human beings, as Paul Zurcher believed it was? How did this belief shape Paul's lifestyle, and how do you think it might have impacted his successes?

3. Paul's mother told him, "You know that you can't out-give the Lord." This early step of "friendship with God" involved a tangible act of trust and sacrifice, based on the belief that God would prove trustworthy and

give back. Is there a tangible step of trust you can take today?

4. What does the phrase "friend of God" mean to you?

5. Paul set apart his basement office, humble as it was, as a place for fellowship with God. He used it to exercise, pray, read, and think. He also had a time set apart for this purpose: the first few hours of every day. Do you have a "space and time" for God in your life? Even a corner of a room, a closet, or five minutes at lunch break can be used. What might be the impact on your life if you chose to set apart a dedicated space and time to seek God's friendship, fellowship, and guidance?

6. Paul committed to reciting each day a prayer written by Heartsill Wilson. Some people prefer to pray their own thoughts, while others use prewritten prayers. Which is your preference? What are the benefits and downsides of these two approaches? How did Wilson's prayer help Paul define and focus his own thoughts and intentions?

7. Stories abound of Paul praying in conference rooms, preparing for business meetings with prayer, and asking God for guidance in every aspect of his business. When asked in his nineties what he did, he said, "I serve God by selling tires." Paul's actions imply a belief that God cares about everything in our lives—even his tire business. Do you believe God cares about your business and the industry you work in? Do you pray like this is true? Take a leap of faith to believe that God cares about the details of your personal and work life, and for one week, pray like it's true. See what happens.

8. Paul's decision to serve on the Taylor board led to significant health benefits for both him and Betty. In fact, he believed it saved his wife's life. Looking back, can you see times when God guided you to make a decision that led to unintended but life-changing consequences?

PRINCIPLE #2

To Develop Effective Relationships

Our relationship with God sets the pattern for all our other relationships. That's why seeking God's friendship, fellowship, and guidance—my first commitment—is so important. What is it that will make the unfaithful man faithful? The controlling man a servant? It is understanding and knowing the living God. It is trusting him to guide you and to give you the power to do his will.

Relationships are built on trust, and trust comes from your inner core, from your character. The most important thing we put into a relationship is our character. Do you know what the most important quality of a leader is? It is character. Character is saying what we mean and meaning what we say, saying it plainly, facing bad news squarely and candidly. Character is being faithful in your actions to your most core values. This inspires trust and develops relationships.

Relationships are also founded on service, on being "others-focused." Service is helping people reach their highest potential. When you choose to serve God, you choose to serve others. If I had to choose the goal that is most important to me, it is service.

A quote often attributed to John Wesley defines a life dedicated to service: "Do all the good you can, by all the means you can, in all the ways you can, as long as you ever can." If you help enough people in this life, they will help you get your heart's greatest desire—a life of no regrets that has brought you closer to God.

— Paul Zurcher, from his 2010 speech,
"Nine Life Commitments"

CHAPTER 2

"We found instead that they first got the right people on the bus, the wrong people off the bus, and the right people in the right seats . . ."

— *Jim Collins[1]*

It was a fine day in the early fifties. Paul and his Firestone representative, Ray Monteith, slid into a corner booth at a local diner.

"Don't even think about getting the check this time, Paul. I'm buying," Ray said with a chuckle and a shake of his head.

Paul laughed and looked over the menu. He knew it almost by heart, so he quickly made his selection and then got down to business. He told Ray, "I'm really torn on the direction to go with the store. I have the tire side, and then I have the fueling station. I feel like I'm juggling the two. I'm not complaining about having too much business, but I feel like I just need to commit to one or the other."

Ray nodded and pulled out a pen. "Well, Paul, you know I'm a tire guy, so you probably know what I'm going to say. You should sell off the fuel business and really focus on selling tires." He started to jot some notes on a napkin.

"I'm just not sure how to go about it," Paul said while Ray continued writing. "If I focus only on tires, I want to know I can be successful at it."

Ray passed the napkin across the table with a bulleted list on it. "I have seen a lot of tire stores come and go. If you do the things on this list, you can't go wrong. Your business will be successful."

This conversation signaled another turning point in the life of Paul Zurcher. After talking with Ray, Paul decided to pour his energy and resources into developing the tire side of his business. Always open to the wise advice of others, he took that napkin business plan and followed it to the nth degree. The rest was tire industry history.

Paul always remembered that Firestone helped him get started, and he remained a faithful supplier of Firestone tires in addition to many other brands. In 2005, he received an award for selling over fifty million Bridgestone Firestone tires and was named the largest Bridgestone Firestone independent tire dealer.

Paul's relationship with Ray Monteith also continued well beyond those early days, growing in depth as the years went by. Ray worked for Firestone for thirteen years and then eventually went into business with Paul. He settled his family in Warsaw, Indiana, and opened Monteith Tire in 1966. Ray's enthusiasm for the business, his family, his faith, and his community was contagious. Eventually Monteith's Best-One Tire and Auto Care grew to include eight locations. Ray always remained a close friend and confidant for Paul.

Paul intentionally partnered with like-minded people such as Ray Monteith. He saw relationships as central to life—and not just any relationships, but *effective* ones. As one of his favorite quotes from leadership expert Jim Collins advised, Paul's goal was to get the right people on the bus, the wrong people off the bus, and the right people in the right seats. He also liked to say he surrounded himself with people smarter than himself and tried to soak up their knowledge and wisdom.

One story clearly illustrates the type of partners Paul chose in business. When Ray Monteith was working at his store in Warsaw, he got a phone call from a college student who needed a set of tires. The student explained how much money he had and the perilous condition of his current tires. Ray assured the young man they could find a used set to fit his budget. The student drove into the store and had all four tires replaced. What the student didn't know until later was that Ray Monteith had actually taken the tires off his own vehicle to give to the young man. This type of servant leadership characterized many of the Best-One partners.

Many similar stories were repeated about Paul quietly taking care of the needs of others. Paul's friend Carolyn Fryback shared one. "This woman was a single mother and she didn't have any money. She had a flat tire, so Zurcher's went out to help her, but she didn't have the money to pay for it. Paul took a look at the rest of her tires and told the guys, 'Just put a whole new set on.'" Carolyn added, "There are lots of stories like that."

Another friend of Paul and Betty, June Amadio, shared a moving story about the lengths the Zurchers willingly went to help a friend. Though June and her husband had moved away from Berne to New York City, Paul and Betty kept in touch and scheduled visits with their longtime friends. One night, June tearfully called Paul and explained that her marriage was falling apart.

Paul immediately said, "June, hold fast. Betty and I will be there tomorrow." They called back later with their travel itinerary, and June met them the following afternoon at the airport. After stopping for a bite to eat, they all returned home, and June and her husband, Dick, pulled up chairs alongside Paul and Betty.

June writes about that night, "Paul had carefully and prayerfully prepared his every word. He would speak a while, then pray with us, give us handwritten notes, and then again speak, read Scripture, have prayer through the entire night until morning. We went out for breakfast and then took them to the airport. That was *intervention* at its best!"

Even though Paul and Betty's encouragement did not save June's marriage, June says she and her ex-husband never forgot that act of love and years later would remember what the experience meant to them both. Paul and Betty were true friends, willing to do whatever it took—even hop on a plane the next day—to be there in a time of need.

Paul understood that every relationship is made up of two. Along with looking for likeminded partners and people he could learn from, he also emphasized the development of his own character so he would be an effective partner and friend to others.

In a speech given later in his life, Paul talked about the phrase "no regrets." "That phrase, 'no regrets,' is an interesting one. You see the phrase painted on skateboards, pasted on the back of cars, and repeated on TV. People talk about living with no regrets, and they generally mean living life to the fullest— but their definition of living life to the fullest may not be the same as ours!"

Paul continued, "On the popular TV show *The Bachelor,* you hear the contestants say 'no regrets' all the time. But I wonder how happy they are. Do you think each of the twenty-five girls dating the one guy is happy? The truth is, our purpose is not to live with no regrets. Our purpose is to be successful. But what is success? It is getting up each morning and saying, 'Lord, what do you want me to do today?' And lying in bed each night saying, 'Lord, I did it.'

"God gives love, joy, and peace—the stuff of 'no regrets'—to people who live successfully. You see, we were created to become like Christ. We were created to know God. Godly behavior—living Christ's values, attitudes, and character—that is our purpose. Said another way, character development is God's purpose for us."

* * *

"Business and Christ-centered action can go together. We have chosen as our core business value caring about people. I say I'm not in the tire business; I'm in the people business!"

— *Paul Zurcher*

Walking into Best-One headquarters in Monroe, Indiana, today, you are clearly visiting a family affair. Paul's office is still there, tucked away in the tight corner he shared with another employee. The desk is narrow, angular, and made of a composite wood. Thick binders on an overhead shelf hold file folders, and a phone is the only real technology at hand.

Paul's son Mark and granddaughter Lindsey have desks a stone's throw away and manage Zurcher's Best-One Tire and Auto Care. Mark and his brother, Larry, serve the Best-One group as advisors and partners. Lindsey is the operations manager of the Monroe location and also supports the group's many partners. Paul's granddaughter Tina works in the same building in the corporate offices. She and her mother, Sue, both act as Best-One attorneys. As I walked the hallways recently, Tina's husband, Mike, emerged from another office to issue a greeting and then return to his work with security and risk management.

Paul's son Larry and grandson Jon travel between the different stores, providing financial feedback and direction. Mark, Larry, Lindsey, and Jon each work with partners to address business-management issues and develop partner and supplier relationships.

The buildings that make up Best-One headquarters—a conglomerate of offices, warehousing space, outdoor storage, and a massive building for servicing transport trucks—sprawl. Zurcher's Best-One Tire is still located in Monroe, Indiana, the town of eight hundred where Paul grew up, and his company takes up more space than anybody expected when he opened his one-bay service shop. It now occupies the old Monroe fire station and several other buildings besides.

Talking to the employees, one gets the impression that even those whose last names aren't Zurcher feel like family. Memories of Paul's business acumen mix with stories of baseball games, barbecues, and chasing Paul through a cornfield in an attempt to throw him in the pool. A cat strolls across the surface of a desk, mostly ignored by the workers—except the one with a paper sign taped to the door that insists the cat be kept out. In an industry that isn't known for long-lasting careers, many of those who work here have been with Zurcher's Best-One Tire for twenty and even thirty years.

Paul began the precedent of incorporating family into his business five decades ago. When he was first starting out, he employed his brother-in-law Weldon as a manager in the store and his sister Gladys in the office. Other siblings worked in varying capacities; his brother Art later worked at the store, his brother Josh worked part-time on Saturdays, and his brother Vernon provided the store's insurance. Old-timers reminisce about how Paul's retired father, Bill, spent most of his days chatting in the waiting room with customers.

When Paul first considered going into business, a number of people told his parents, "That son of yours is taking too much risk. This town is too small and can't support a business." Then they said, "Tell Paul never to take any family into the business, because that's trouble too." With a chuckle, Paul often reflected on that advice, saying, "I guess I wasn't a very good listener."

Even Paul's wife, Betty, supported the business in key ways. In addition to raising their three children, Betty came in to the store and helped with bookkeeping and phone calls. At one point, when she and Paul were out on their weekly date night, Betty asked if they could hire someone to help with the housework so she could work more at the store. Atypically for that era, Paul readily agreed. He enjoyed working alongside his wife. Even into her seventies, Betty spent time at the store each day sorting and delivering the mail to the employees.

As Paul continued to expand Best-One, his responsibilities increased, and he had to spend more time on the road. When asked if she ever became frustrated with his time away, however, Betty just responded, "I can't keep him all to myself. People need him." She knew Paul was a gift and she needed to share that gift with others.

Jay Kesler, president emeritus of Taylor University, remembers, "They were true partners in life and in the business, and they enjoyed it." Even when Betty's memory started to fade later in life, this connection remained strong. Betty's Alzheimer's progressed to a point where she only recognized and knew Paul. In the care of loving nurses at Swiss Village in Berne, each day she anxiously asked for Paul and awaited his return. Despite his many responsibilities, Paul rushed back each day to see Betty, eat dinner with her, and stay with her until she went to bed.

Paul's granddaughter Jackie once accompanied Paul on one of these visits to Swiss Village. She remembers Betty saying as she climbed into bed, "Paul, I'm so scared." Paul sat on the edge of Betty's bed, tucked the blankets tightly around her, and gently rubbed his finger along her cheek. "Everything will be okay," he told her, repeating those words until Betty drifted off to sleep. Paul was Betty's lifeline in an increasingly hazy and confusing world.

Jackie said about this glimpse into her grandparents' lives, "It was a reminder to not waste moments with loved ones; every second is precious and an opportunity to show love, comfort, and compassion. There are these blessed moments, which are gifts that transform your life. Grandpa was a vehicle for God. His heart was open, and he desired to do God's will, and God worked beautifully through him!"

Because Betty would become anxious when he was away, Paul had the idea to write a letter to Betty that the nurses could read to her when she asked for him. This is what the letter said:

Dearest Betty,

I want to remind you how very special and important you are to me, and that I love you very much.

I look forward to seeing you in just a little bit. I am at work today and am traveling to some of our stores. Rest assured that I will be back this evening, and that I will come to see you then. I look forward to spending time with you very soon!

You are okay, you are safe, and you are with people right now who care about you very much. You have nothing to be concerned or worried about. I promise that I will be there with you soon! Everything is just fine.

Remember that I love you very much and want you to enjoy your day!

Love,

Paul

In 2015 when Paul was hospitalized, his main motivation for getting well was to return to Betty and care for her. He was frail, yet he kept saying, "I need to get my energy back. I have to get back to Mom."

Their daughter, Colleen, recalls how the day Paul died the family agreed not to tell Betty because of her advanced Alzheimer's. Strangely, though, that very day Betty stopped asking for Paul—something she had done without ceasing since he entered the hospital. Somehow, it was as if she knew in her spirit he had gone ahead of her to heaven.

When Paul passed out of this world, Colleen said, "I felt like God was saying to Dad, 'You don't have to worry about Betty anymore. I will take care of her and bring her to you.'" Betty died less than a year later, and it was a time of bittersweet rejoicing. She was in the presence of her Savior, joyfully reunited with Paul, and made whole once again. Because of the depth of their love for one another, their family had known Paul and Betty couldn't be apart for long.

* * *

"People are the prime reason for any business success or failure. So if you build your people, you build your business."

— *Paul Zurcher*

It was 2005. Paul strode into the office of Jim Channell, director of retail development at Southern Indiana Tire. He enthusiastically shook Jim's hand and began to ask him about his family and the business. Before they sat down to go over the year's financials, Jim grabbed the latest issue of *Modern Tire Dealer* from his desk. The front cover featured a large photo of Paul with the byline, "Character Counts: Paul Zurcher, Tire Dealer of the Year." This coveted distinction had been earlier bestowed on other tire gurus, like the owners of Tire Rack and Discount Tire.

"Autograph this for me, will you, Paul?" Jim asked, handing him his copy of the magazine. Paul chuckled and promptly signed the cover. He laid the magazine on Jim's desk, and the two men got down to business.

The next day Jim picked up the magazine and for the first time looked at what Paul had written. It said, "To MY Tire Dealer of the Year. Paul Zurcher." Jim wrote about this moment, "Typical of Paul, he turned the moment to shine the light on me rather than himself."

Paul received many such awards, but instead of accepting all the praise, he credited his family and the people around him. On Paul's ninetieth birthday, his family and a few close friends surprised him for lunch at a local restaurant, the Back 40. Even more surprising, the area's state representative, Matt Lehman, was also present. Before the meal began, Matt called Paul in front of everyone and presented him with the Sagamore of the Wabash, the highest distinction in Indiana bestowed by the governor. At first Paul was speechless, but he quickly began to pay tribute to Betty, his family, his friends, and his partners.

When Paul passed away, Rep. Matt Lehman reflected on that day. He was quoted in the local newspaper saying, "What I took from Paul's life was that he's always been such a humble person. Even when he was being recognized for his accomplishments, he deferred to others. He had such a servant's heart."

Another example of Paul's humility took place at the annual Best-One seminar. Each year Paul gave a speech to the hundreds of partners and employees gathered for an awards dinner.

More often than not a standing ovation followed his speech. Paul would smile, enjoying everyone's enthusiasm, but then he would begin to thank the partners and their families. Larry said, "Every seminar, Dad would be sure to thank the spouses who were behind the partners—to talk about how important they were to the success of the business. And he was always thankful for Mom and how she supported him."

Paul's attitude of humility and gratitude, and the time and focus he put into his family and business relationships, were not accidental. He made choices to live and think this way.

"Effective people, at their core, are thinking people," Paul said in a speech to the Adams Central School Board in 2008. "They regularly analyze their actions to determine where they are on the path to their objectives (and whether the path they're on is the right one). To do this, we have two tools we can rely on, two tools that are entirely under our control. They are our attitudes and our actions.

"You've all heard about stimulus and response. Remember Pavlov's dog? The famous scientist spent hours ringing a bell and then dropping a treat to the dog. After a while, the dog would start to salivate when the bell was rung—before he saw the treat.

"So a stimulus produces a response. But, for us, something is missing. The missing link is Choice. In that second between stimulus and response, you have a choice. You can choose to be reactive, or you can choose to be proactive. In that second, you make your choice. The choice carries the consequences. One way to look at this is to put a new spin on the word *responsibility*. Think of it as two words—response and ability. Proactive people develop the ability to choose their response. So they act in accordance with their values and decisions, not their moods and conditions."

Though Paul did receive much recognition during his lifetime, most of his acts of service went unnoticed. People would not know how Paul bought a car for someone who needed one but could not afford it, or how he loaned money to neighbors and employees in a tight spot. Quite often the money was not repaid in full, but Paul did not become bitter. He considered it a privilege to come alongside others during difficult times.

> *"Proactive people develop the ability to choose their response. So they act in accordance with their values and decisions, not their moods and conditions."*
> — *Paul Zurcher*

Paul and Betty's good friends, Ron and Carolyn Fryback and Sharlene Lehman from Berne, shared how Paul and Betty came to the aid of anyone in need at their church or in the community. Carolyn said, "They never wanted any praise. But between the two of them, if you had a problem and something was needed, they made sure somebody was there, and usually it was them." They supported a woman in the church who had cancer, donated a beautiful Christmas tree and nativity for the church, and gave a car to a teenage boy who was working but could not afford one. Over and over, Paul and Betty made the choice to put people first—to serve them, to care about them, to show them love.

At Paul's funeral, one gentleman from Monroe shared how his family had gone through a trying time many years earlier. His wife was hospitalized for weeks after surviving a serious car accident. The man found himself stretched to the limit as he tried to keep his job and spend time with his wife at the hospital. Often he only had time to run home, shower, and change before he hurried back to his wife. On one of these trips home, he opened the bare refrigerator and noticed a meat tray and other items he hadn't purchased. Puzzled, he gratefully ate some of the food before driving back to the hospital.

This went on for many weeks. The man wondered who was bringing him this food and began to suspect Paul and Betty, who lived just down the street. In those days, no one in Monroe locked their doors, so they could have dropped the food off while he was out. Finally, one day at the tire store the man asked Paul about the food. Paul just smiled and didn't say a thing.

Even fifty years later, the Monroe man choked up telling the story. Paul and Betty saw a need and met it. Sometimes they received awards and ceremonies, but more often than not their deeds were noticed only by God and those whose lives they touched.

Questions to Ponder

Principle #2: To Develop Effective Relationships

1. Paul believed "relationships are built on trust, and trust comes from your inner core, from your character. The most important thing we put into a relationship is our character." When we talk about relationships, we often think of the other person first. But Paul believed that if we are to develop effective relationships, we need to start with ourselves—by becoming trustworthy people. Is this a principle you take seriously in your life? Do you actively work on becoming a person of character? If not, what are some practical steps you could take to improve this area of your life? Looking at Paul's Nine Life Principles, what are

some commitments you could make that would help you in this area?

2. Paul said, "Character is being faithful in your actions to your most core values. This inspires trust and develops relationships." This suggests that to be a person of character, we must know ourselves. What are your core values? Can you define them? Are they written down? Do you live them out? What areas of compromise can you identify in your life where you are *not* living out your core values? How would it impact your life to live them out more faithfully?

3. After character, Paul believed "relationships are also founded on service, on being 'others-focused.' Service is helping people reach their highest potential." Is this different from how you have thought about service before? Look at the people who surround you in family, work, and community. What is their highest potential? What could you do in word, act, or investment to help them reach it?

4. Early in his career, Paul expressed frustration at feeling torn between two sides of his business. His friend advised him to focus on the tire business. Are you experiencing frustration in any area of your life? Is there a friend or mentor whose help you could seek out? Specifically, where might you need to let one "good" thing go in order to focus on the best?

5. Paul resonated with Jim Collins's quote about getting the "right people on the bus" and the "wrong people off the bus." Paul intentionally partnered with like-minded people. He actively sought out people who were going the same direction in life and getting there in the same way. Are you strategic about the people you partner with, in business or elsewhere? What are the criteria that make some people "right" and others "wrong" for partnership with you?

6. Paul intentionally hired members of his own family, and he deliberately fostered a family atmosphere throughout the company. Do you see this as wise or foolish? What are the potential upsides and downsides of working with family? How can the pitfalls be guarded against? On the flip side, what are the benefits of fostering a "family feel" within a company? How could you foster this spirit among the people you lead?

7. Paul purposely surrounded himself with people "smarter than himself" and sought out advice and wisdom from others, but he also knew when not to listen. When in early years he was told that owning a business was too much risk, that his town could never support a business, and that he should never hire family, he ignored the comments and went ahead with his decisions according to his own core values. Do you see the "right people and wrong people" principle in action here? How do you discern who and what to listen to, and who and what to set aside?

8. Paul's relationship with his wife, Betty, was the most important of his life next to his relationship with God. Jay Kesler said of them that they were "true partners in life and in the business, and they enjoyed it." Can this be said of your marriage? The Zurchers' marriage had its challenges, but their shared faith, commitment, and give-and-take allowed them to build something lasting and strong. Paul also recognized the importance of this relationship to others. His son Larry said, "Dad would be sure to thank the spouses who were behind the partners—to talk about how important they were to the success of the business." Have you recognized the impact of your marriage on the rest of your life, especially work and business? What can you do

to prioritize your relationship with your spouse and build a healthy, strong relationship?

9. When he was praised, Paul passed the credit on to others. Rather than false humility, this reflected his perception of life and the world: everything was a gift, he had received as much as he had given, and he would not be where he was without the help of others. Do you share this perspective? Why or why not? If you have never thought about life this way, what happens if you try to look at life through this lens of gratitude? How might it change the way you feel and act today?

PRINCIPLE #3

To Treat Everyone with Honor, Love, Dignity, and Respect

Caring is the foundation of everything. How much we care about others determines everything we do.

There's a story about a father and son walking down a beach. Thousands of starfish had been stranded by the tide and were suffocating. The boy grabbed one starfish and flung it back into the sea. His father said, "You know there are thousands more here. Throwing one back doesn't mean much." The son replied, "It meant everything to that one."

To have a great life, start loving—love God, other people, yourself, just start somewhere! Your love will grow as you love. We are put on this earth to love the Lord, to love others, to love life, and live it abundantly! How you think about love will determine how you live all your days.

The point of life is learning to love. The top three-point formula for living is in this immortal verse: "And now these three remain: faith, hope, and love. But the greatest of these is love" (1 Corinthians 13:13). Here are three powerful life-lifters: Faith, the power that moves mountains; Hope, the attitude of expectancy that the best is yet to be; and Love, a heart of caring, compassion, and understanding—the greatest power of all. Christian love gives deep joy.

— Paul Zurcher, from his 2010 speech,
"Nine Life Commitments"

CHAPTER 3

"Do all the good you can, by all the means you can, in all the ways you can, in all the places you can, at all the times you can, to all the people you can, as long as you ever can."

— *Attributed to John Wesley*

Paul was just about to climb into bed when the phone on the nightstand rang. He glanced at the clock. Ten p.m. The phone kept ringing, and Paul rushed to answer it before it woke up Betty or the kids.

"Hello?" He listened for a minute. "It's no trouble. I will be over in about five minutes."

Paul threw a shirt and pants over his pajamas and drove to the tire store. A teenage boy and girl sheepishly stood next to their car and the gas pump. Smiling, Paul unlocked the door to the store, turned on a few lights, and flipped on the pumps.

The boy quickly filled his car with about four dollars' worth of gas and paid Paul. "We're so sorry we had to call you," the girl said. "We were driving home from a basketball game in Bluffton and didn't have enough gas to get home." Both the boy and girl thanked Paul many times over before driving away.

Chuckling, Paul closed up the store and headed back home. This wasn't a nightly occurrence, but he often got calls in the middle of the night about a flat tire or a car out of gas. He would go in himself and take care of the customer, no matter the time. Paul couldn't have known, however, that in this case it was a special young lady he had just helped. Years later his son Larry would marry Sue Schurger, and she never forgot Paul's kindness.

Paul's faithful service built a flock of loyal Zurcher Tire customers. People from over an hour away drove to the small town of Monroe, refusing to buy their tires anywhere else. They enjoyed the playful banter with the salesmen and the consistent, quality service, which often went above and beyond.

One day a young boy accompanied his father into the tire store. Paul greeted them warmly and immediately noticed the boy's Cincinnati Reds hat. With a twinkle in his eye, Paul asked the boy, "How would you like to go to a Reds game?" He brought the boy and his father back to his desk and gave them a set of tickets to a game of their choice. Paul owned season tickets to the Reds for over ten years and enjoyed giving them away almost as much as attending the games with his family.

Like his customers, Paul's employees also felt deep loyalty to their boss. Many spent their entire careers working at Zurcher Tire. One employee remembered how Paul used to offer to buy a steak dinner for anyone willing to take a late farm call on a Saturday afternoon. Rather than demanding an employee answer the call, Paul understood his employees and motivated them in a good-natured way. Larry said, "I think Dad ended up buying a lot of steak dinners!"

Another employee, Bobby Hurst, also recalls Paul's Reds tickets. When he and Paul worked late, Paul might suddenly say, "I've got tickets for tonight's Reds game. Wanna go?" Cincinnati was a good three-hour drive, but Paul was rumored to make the trip in almost half that. (There was a reason the Best-One group had T-shirts made with a cartoon of Paul sitting at traffic school!) They would drive straight there, watch the game, and drive back late at night. Of course, they were both at work again bright and early the next day. Though they might have been tired, Paul's employees did not forget his generosity and kindness.

* * *

"Trust is the glue of life. It is the glue that holds organizations, cultures, and relationships together. Ironically it comes from the speed of going slow. With people, fast is slow and slow is fast."

— *Stephen R. Covey[1]*

"Paul and Betty have had a profound impact on my wife and me throughout the last forty-four years," writes John Enright. He and his wife, Kendra, have served faithfully as missionaries in Africa for their entire lives. John continues, "They were dear friends, committed Christian coworkers, and an inspiration throughout our years of working in Africa."

Paul and Betty first heard the Enrights speak in 1972 at the First United Methodist Church in Bluffton, Indiana. Paul later shared with them that he had wanted to invest some money in the stock market at the time but instead decided to invest the money in this young couple going out onto the missionary field. "He believed that investing in people would give a higher return on his money," John says.

Shortly before Paul's death, the Enrights met Paul in Noblesville, Indiana, and Paul reminded John of that first decision to support them as missionaries. Paul assured the couple that he felt his investment in Kendra and John had been the best investment he could have made. John reflects, "Kendra and I have worked for forty-three years in Africa and seen many accomplishments. The Zurchers were partners with us always and share in those accomplishments."

John's words are modest; by many standards, the Enrights' work has been astonishing. They credit some surprising sources for their inspiration. "One of the most important things Paul has done for me," John says, "was to give me the business model that I am currently using with over twelve thousand African villagers who are involved in agricultural projects in both Zambia and Congo. We are primarily working in the area of producing honey at this time but will also be branching out into livestock and crops. Paul explained to me how he set up partnerships with families based on character and commitment. He went into great detail on how he set up these partnerships. I have been able to take that model and, inspired by his success, find a way to establish a similar model here in Africa. The project is going forward well, and we hope in the future to introduce this concept all over Africa as we work with impoverished villagers and small-scale farmers using a micro-franchise model based on Paul's business model in America."

While supporting the Enrights, Paul and Betty did much more than write a monthly check. At one point, Paul sent a container-load of tires to Africa to help in their work.

John also remembers conducting two three-day seminars at a conference center in North America about the kingdom of God; Paul attended every session despite his busy schedule.

Once when he was in Pendleton, Indiana, buying tires, John began talking to the owner of the store. By way of making conversation, he said, "I have a friend in the tire business. His name is Paul Zurcher."

The man stopped, turned to John, and said with awe, "You know Paul?" He proceeded to tell John the story of how Paul had not only made it possible for him to be in business, but had helped lead him to a relationship with the Lord. John agreed wholeheartedly with the man that Paul was a blessing to all he met.

The Enrights witnessed how, rather than simply providing capital, Paul came alongside others and partnered with them to be successful. Whether in Africa or rural Indiana, people flourish when they are treated with honor, love, dignity, and respect.

* * *

"Before you can do anything that touches the lives of others, you must show them honor, love, dignity, and respect. Without that, there can be no connection, no trust, and no future together."

— *Paul Zurcher*

Sitting at a table with four other tire dealers, Paul placed his order. Nothing fancy—they were just getting a quick bite to eat before their meetings began. The waitress smiled and nodded as the orders were placed rather than writing them on her notepad. She returned promptly with the meals, and each was prepared exactly to their specifications.

As she passed out the meals, Paul said, "You have quite a talent there, young lady. I have never had such wonderful service before."

The girl ducked her head and thanked Paul for his compliment.

"I am serious, you are very talented. What are you hoping to do with your life?"

Surprised by his genuine interest, she confided, "I would like to own my own restaurant someday."

Paul and the other dealers encouraged her to pursue her dream. "I will be one of your first customers," Paul promised.

A year later Paul returned to the same restaurant and spotted the same waitress across the room. He tapped her on the shoulder and said, "I don't know if you remember me, but you were our waitress about a year ago and did a fantastic job."

The girl's face immediately lit up, and she gushed, "Of course I remember you! You were the one who said I should open my own restaurant. I've started saving so I can do that someday."

Paul again commended her on her service and encouraged her to keep following her dream.

Paul not only took great joy in fulfilling his dreams, but he also wanted to help others accomplish theirs. He really *saw* and valued each person he came in contact with.

At times Paul perceived someone's potential before they even realized it. Rick Hursell and his wife, Tammy, explained such a time when Rick came to be the manager of Best-One Tire of Angola. Rick had been working as a mechanic in the store when Paul approached him about managing it. Rick turned Paul down a number of times but finally relented.

Rick remembers, "After so many times telling Paul Zurcher no, I realized he wasn't going to take no for an answer. But we did the right thing, and I appreciate the opportunity to be blessed to run the store and that he had the confidence in me to do what needed to be done. He gave me that confidence, and he encouraged me. I only wish we had done it sooner! I felt very blessed."

As Rick grew into his role as a manager, Paul served as his mentor. Rick says, "Paul Zurcher accepted you and made you feel important and gave you the confidence to do anything. I looked up to him, and he was someone very special in my heart. To this day, I still think of what Paul would do when I'm in a tough situation. He was almost a father figure that I didn't have, because I lost my parents when I was thirteen. If anything, I wish I'd met him sooner in life."

Over the years, Rick and Tammy's family developed a special relationship with Paul. They shared many meals together at the local Back 40 restaurant, and Paul always made it a point to attend their company Christmas party. With tears in her eyes, Tammy thinks back on her conversations with Paul. "He accepted me for me. I'm pretty outspoken, and he just accepted me for me. He said, 'Don't you change. Just always be yourself.' He took me and he understood me, and he liked me for me. I loved that about him."

The Hursells, as well as many other individuals and couples, could tell Paul truly cared. He wanted others to succeed, not just for the sake of the business, but also to see them exercise their God-given talents.

Jay Kesler, president emeritus of Taylor University, sees this as one of the key qualities that set Paul apart. "There are managers and business owners who see people more or less as things, units. Paul was a people person. He knew that the success of his business was directly related to how happy and satisfied his employees were. He knew they were the key. And his business formula of having managers who had skin in the game was the same way—he wanted managers who owned something. His success was the people."

John Gamauf, former president of Consumer Tires, Bridgestone Firestone, remembers the experience of calling Paul's office. "When I call a dealer, a receptionist asks, 'Who's calling?' When I called into Monroe, Indiana, and I asked for Paul Zurcher, nobody there ever asked who was calling. His calls were never screened, and within fifteen seconds you would hear, 'Hello, this is Paul speaking.' Such a personal thing today that we are losing in business."

In Jay Kesler's view, Paul's emphasis on people went much deeper than a general life philosophy. It was integrally connected to his Christian faith. "He *practiced* the gospel in his relationships. Many businessmen are honest. Many are very smart, very fair. It's even in the literature—it's popular to talk about how your people are the center of your business. But to many, that's a mantra, it's a method, it's a technique. To Paul it was not a mantra, not a method, not a technique. He actually *believed* it because it was endemic in his Christianity.

"You see, it naturally came out of his interpretation of a Christian. He knew that Jesus was not a respecter of persons, so a man who is loading a truck in the back of a warehouse is a human being, is a unique creation of the Holy God just like you.

"I meet so many people giving lectures about leadership, lectures about management, and they're talking about technique. This is not a strategy, not a technique, not a formula. It is something you believe or don't believe. From a Christian viewpoint, if you stuck a fork in Paul, he's done in the middle the same way he's done at the edges. He actually was interested in you. That's not unusual in families, but for a man as busy and as successful as he was, many times those people are preoccupied. They've got a lot on their minds."

Paul summed up this value well in a speech to a group of business leaders. "I have a last thought on how we should treat our customers, associates, and suppliers. Trust becomes a verb when you show people their worth and potential so clearly that they are inspired to see it in themselves."

An email from Jim Jones, a Best-One partner, proves the truth of Jay's assessment of Paul. "I have two stories I never forgot. The first is one of the proudest moments of my life. It happened with Paul a few years ago. We were at a Bridgestone cocktail function, and I asked him to come over to introduce him to my wife. I believed (incorrectly) that he would not remember meeting her previously. Not only did he extend his hand to her and say 'Hello, Jennifer' before I could, he then said something I will never forget. He said, 'I want you to know something; you have a real winner here in this man next to you. He is first class and someone I am proud to be a partner with.'

"It still brings a tear to my eye that Paul Zurcher said that about me, little ol' me. I decided right then and there I would never do anything to let him down—ever! He had such a way of building you up, no matter what was going on.

> *"Trust becomes a verb when you show people their worth and potential so clearly that they are inspired to see it in themselves."*
> *— Paul Zurcher*

"The second one was just a few years ago at the Churchill Downs event. In the middle of all the festivities, I approached him just to say hello. In the middle of everything else, he asked how I was doing with a little trademark legal issue we were having. It never ceased to amaze me how he kept track of so many little details."

Anyone who knew Paul would say it wasn't details he kept track of, but people. Paul cared, and everyone knew it. For many, their lives were changed by it.

Questions to Ponder

Principle #3: To Treat Everyone with Honor, Love, Dignity, and Respect

1. In Paul's speech, he said, "Caring is the foundation of everything. How much we care about others determines everything we do." Do you agree with this? How do you see this idea that "caring is the foundation of everything" playing out—negatively or positively—in the lives and businesses around you? Think back on your own life. How

did the care of another person impact your life? Are you paying that forward?

2. Paul also said, "To have a great life, start loving—love God, other people, yourself, just start somewhere!" Who do you love? What do you love? Do you love life? Do you enjoy it? Why or why not? How could you begin to make love—for God, others, yourself, and life itself—more central to the way you think and act every day?

3. Paul's faithful service built a flock of loyal Zurcher Tire customers. Like his customers, Paul's employees also felt deep loyalty to their boss. Many worked at Zurcher Tire for their entire careers. We do not often link the idea of love with the idea of business, yet it seems clear that a simple principle like always treating others with love—with dignity, honor, and respect—can have a profound impact on business. How might it impact your life and business to implement this principle in a greater way today?

4. Sometimes we may think that "love" always means something big and grandiose—a huge sacrifice or an intense emotional experience. But Paul showed love in thousands of small simple ways. Whether with Reds tickets or a simple question and word of encouragement to a waitress, Paul dignified the lives of others and helped them have fun and fulfill their dreams. He would say that was love in action. Rather than trying to do something enormous today, what small thing can you do to show someone respect, honor, and love today? What might the compound effect of a lifetime of doing this be?

5. John Enright shared how Paul "believed that investing in people would give a higher return on his money." When you look at the number of lives John and Kendra Enright

were able to touch and the economic impact they have had in southern Africa, would you agree with Paul's assessment? Why or why not?

6. The Enrights witnessed how Paul came alongside others, rather than only providing capital, and partnered with them to be successful. We are often encouraged to give money to charity, but providing capital is not the only way to benefit others. What avenues of partnership are open to you that can empower and help other people, besides the giving of finances? What creative impact can you have?

7. Jay Kesler said that for many people, the idea that people are the center of your business is "a mantra, it's a method, it's a technique." For Paul, Jay says, this idea was not just a technique because it played a central role in his entire belief system, his Christianity. How do you respond to the idea that people are the center of your business? Is this something you truly believe and live out? Why or why not?

Principle #4

To Be Self-Disciplined and Self-Controlled

It takes discipline and self-control to focus your life. Only the disciplined get really good at anything.

Let me tell you a story about the day I quit golf. I placed my tee down and took a swing. The tee happened to be next to an anthill, and ants went flying everywhere, but the ball just sat on the tee. My golf partners politely looked the other way. I took another swing, and more dead ants shot through the air. There were only two live ants left. One looked at the other and said, "Quick, get on the ball!" That's the day I decided I did not have the self-discipline to be good at golf.

Anyone who is really good at something has worked hard at it, and hard work requires self-discipline. It all comes down to two questions—what do you want out of life, and are you willing to pay the price?

Knowing your purpose focuses your life. Without purpose, you keep aimlessly changing directions, hoping for fulfillment. It might be a life of "no regrets" by some people's measure, but not by ours as Christians. It takes self-discipline and self-control to "keep your eye on the prize" and seek to know God through all your thoughts and actions.

How do you develop self-discipline and self-control? I read a book once that outlined five steps. The first step is to Commit—commit to the Lord and to his path for you. The second step is to Pray—ask the Lord to share his strength. The third step is to Choose—choose to do what God wants you to do. The fourth step is to Identify— decide what values you want to govern your life. And the fifth step is to Prioritize—focus on the most important items first. There's no getting around it: self-discipline and self-control are essential to a successful life.

— Paul Zurcher, from his 2010 speech,
"Nine Life Commitments"

CHAPTER 4

"In a time of drastic change it is the learners who inherit the future. The learned usually find themselves equipped to live in a world that no longer exists."

— *Eric Hoffer[1]*

Sitting in his home office, Paul pulled out his highlighter and pad of sticky notes. He had read through this book twice before and scribbled some notes in the margin. Now he wanted to read it again and mark his favorite quotes. He sighed contentedly as he sat back in his recliner and began to read.

From the age of twenty-two, this scene replayed in Paul's life over and over. When Paul came back from the service he was challenged to set life goals in five categories: mental, spiritual, physical, family, and financial. For his mental goal, Paul chose to read on average an hour and a half each day. He also spent that time listening to books on tape or motivational speakers. He kept to this commitment no matter his schedule or obligations. One Best-One partner, Greg Aspy, remembers seeing Paul reading at Firestone's One Hundredth Anniversary in Las Vegas. While others played slots and enjoyed drinks, Paul sat in a quiet corner reading a motivational book. He said that was so typical of Paul.

In a talk given to college students years later, Paul recalled making the choice to give reading a prominent place in his life. "After the war, I didn't know what the future would hold. One day, a friend of mine told me he thought I could be successful in business. About the same time, I read a book called *Life Is Tremendous* by Charlie 'Tremendous' Jones.

"At that point, much as you are doing now, I took a long, hard look at my future. God had given me some tools—I had to take it from there, with his help! I decided to live life wide open, to expand my mind and welcome possibilities. Thanks to God and Mr. Jones, I made a commitment to spend an hour and a half each day feeding my mind, by reading books, talking with people. This simple commitment is a road map for life!"

Jones wrote, "Readers are not necessarily leaders, but leaders are almost always readers."[2] He encouraged others to read with the purpose of applying lessons learned to life and sharing them with others. Paul did exactly that. He was not interested in head knowledge but in lessons that would impact his life.

Paul not only read books but reread them. He made notes in the margins, highlighted in different colors, and marked pages with sticky notes. Once when he was given a book to read, he sheepishly said a few weeks later, "I hope that was to keep," because he had marked up all the pages.

Paul mainly read books about business, leadership, or faith. He was genuinely curious as to why people would read fiction books for fun. To him, books were direct means to stretch his mind and grow, and he read from very specific genres.

In addition to the Bible, other important books in Paul's life included *The Purpose Driven Life* by Rick Warren, *30 Life Principles* by Charles Stanley, *The Seven Habits of Highly Effective People* and *The Eighth Habit* by Stephen R. Covey, *Good to Great* by Jim Collins, and *See You at the Top* by Zig Ziglar. Paul's copies of these books are literally falling to pieces from rereading over the years. When reading any of these books, you can pick out bits of Paul in them—his favorite quotes, his goals, and his habits. More than anyone I know, Paul read these books and actually did what they said. He *did* live a purposeful life, abide by his principles, cultivate lifelong habits, and pursue excellence as these books outline.

Jay Kesler of Taylor University recalls that one of his first connection points with Paul was their mutual love for books. Kesler explains, "Paul as a businessman was a rather unusual person in the sense that he actually read books. One of my hobbies is presidential biography, and I have half a dozen biographies of Lyndon Johnson, for instance. Lyndon Johnson was nobody's fool, of course, but he confessed once that he had never finished a book after he graduated from college. He had started many books, got the idea of them, but he never finished one; he was just too busy. I've found that many people don't read books. They maybe buy a book at the airport, and they read a chapter, but Paul read books. A little later I discovered most of his books were about business, but he did read other things. We both felt you could learn by reading."

For Paul, reading was a discipline indeed. Shelves and boxes of books in his office today—extensively marked up with his wobbly handwriting—testify to his commitment to lifelong learning. His favorite books were those you could really *practice,* principles and attitudes that would go to work for you if you went to work with them.

But, Jay remembers, self-discipline didn't end with reading. "Of course he got his exercise. He believed that keeping his body in shape was part of his spiritual duty, and he did that.

"I had a little slogan Paul liked: 'I slept and dreamt that life was joy. I woke and found that life was duty. I do my duty, and God gives me joy.' Paul got his joy out of doing his duty. And I think God put his hand on Paul's shoulder and said 'Well done, good and faithful servant.' I think that was the great joy of his life. Joy is different than fun. Joy is deeper than fun. Did Paul golf? I think Paul would rather spend time with Betty. Going out for dinner with her afterward would be more fun to him than going out to play golf with three or four men. He was family oriented."

Whether through reading, exercising, or following his other life goals, Paul received joy from living his life purposefully for the Lord. He saw self-discipline both as a byproduct and a driver of purpose.

* * *

"And yet in our world everybody thinks of changing humanity, and nobody thinks of changing himself."

— *Leo Tolstoy*[3]

When you ask longtime Best-One partner Paul Weaver what was unusual about his friend Paul Zurcher, he says, "Paul was the best I've ever seen at never letting his emotions get to him. He always kept his emotions controlled. That has rubbed off on me: don't let things affect *me*. Once you learn that no one can affect you, you have more control of your stuff. It's you, it's not them. People can call you names, they can do everything in the book, *but they can't control you unless you let them.* That's something that sticks with me all the time."

Business is a melting pot of people with varying personalities, standards, needs, and goals—so it's a natural breeding ground for conflict. Both Paul Zurcher and Paul Weaver experienced plenty of it over the years.

Paul Weaver remembers many a typical board meeting: "Paul [Zurcher] kept the focus on issues, not on people. I can love you, but I don't have to like what you did or the way you did it. Over the years we've had a lot of conflicts. I think about a lot of them, and I didn't always handle them very well. But Paul seemed to come out with the results that we had talked about beforehand. We'd ask, 'What do we really want to see happen in this meeting,' and somehow we got there or we planted the seed. He'd always say, 'Well, Paul, we planted a seed, now let's see if it sprouts.' And that's all you can do a lot of times when you have a partner."

Weaver laughs. "You can't go in there with a hammer and say this is the way you're gonna do it, because they will do it that way just to prove it won't work. But if you get buy-in and they agree to it, if somehow you get them to *see* it, it'll flourish.

"I've had this happen: We'd talk to a person or a manager and we'd plant that seed, and a few months later he'd come on back and say, 'I've been thinking about what you guys said in that meeting, and I think it's gonna work.' And then he would tell me how he's gonna make it work. So seeds do grow. I mean, you think about it, that's what we do with our kids, we plant seeds and watch them grow. Paul's way of doing things was always just outstanding. I learned so much from him."

John Gamauf of Bridgestone Firestone remembers Paul's unusual cool in a meeting where he had every right to become angry and lose control. "What had happened was there was the merger between Bridgestone and Firestone, so Best-One was our largest customer, and we negotiated prices. Back then, you did it at the end of the last quarter and then it was good for the whole year. That was the agreement, that you would never change the pricing.

"Well, new management came in from Bridgestone and I got a new boss, and he was going to show Paul how tough he was, I guess. He decided we were going to change Best-One's buying price just a few months into the new year. I said, 'We can't do that. We have already given him our word that this is the buying price for the whole year.' My new boss said, 'No, no, no, we are going to change this pricing now. Set up a meeting.' So I called Paul and told him, 'I'm really uncomfortable here. My new boss wants to change your buying price effective immediately.'

"So we set up the meeting and you could cut the air with a knife. It was tense. Besides Paul, Mark Zurcher, Paul Swentzel, and Tom Kiehfuss, the regional manager and close friend were also present. We are sitting in the meeting and this new boss tells Paul how he is changing the buying price for Best-One effective immediately. The price difference was not a couple of thousand dollars; it was in the multi-million-dollar range of difference. So, Paul has all of these partners he is responsible for. You know if I would have been in this same meeting, ninety-nine out of a hundred tire dealers would have been screaming and yelling and all upset.

"Paul, he just took it all in, and I think sometimes he got into a meditative state when he was thinking. He wouldn't really let on exactly what he was feeling and thinking. He was taking it all in. After this bad news hit, he always had this little binder he would write notes in. He closed up his binder, and he put it into his briefcase. I remember the sound of him opening and closing his briefcase. He put his pen inside, and after he closed it, he put his hands on top of his briefcase. Then he looked everyone in the eyes, and all he said was, 'Gentlemen, this meeting is over.'

"It was the coolest thing I ever saw! I call it his 'Cool Hand Luke' or 'Dirty Harry' moment. The bottom line is that our business fell ten million dollars that year because my new boss made a stupid decision, thinking he was going to push Paul around. Paul did it quietly, but his message got across. We never ever did anything like that again. It was just the way Paul handled himself in his meetings. Even though it was the worst news he could have gotten, he was respectful. I thought it was brilliant."

Stories about Paul Zurcher highlight the interplay of intentionality, self-discipline, and seeing results. His unusual intentionality about life—especially his values—coupled with a close walk with God fueled his ability to remain focused, self-controlled, and caring.

For both Paul Zurcher and Paul Weaver, values drove business, and values couldn't be lived out without discipline and the ability to manage oneself first. "Customers first" is one value that takes self-discipline and a higher purpose to achieve. It's just one of the core beliefs that drove business for both men. Their commitment to their partners was another.

Paul Weaver says, "I've chosen the model, like Paul and Ray, of the partnerships. They went out and found good people who had the entrepreneurial spirit and wanted to be successful. Instead of me owning everything, I've got partners—over twenty partners. There are good points and there are bad points to having partners. But I believe when a guy owns a piece of the pie, they take pride in their store and what they do.

"And I believe in really finding the right people and training them. To me, you get personal. A guy with a positive attitude, you can train him. But if you've got a guy with a bad attitude, you can't train him. If they question and fight you on everything, there's nothing you can do."

Paul Zurcher's dual commitment to people and to integrity paid off in many ways. The Weavers and Zurchers developed a close working relationship founded on these principles.

"Both families want to do the right thing for the business, and for the employees, and for the customers. You always come back to 'Do the right things right.' I heard that from Paul over and over again. The whole family's that way. That's what we all want to get done. It's not about me; it's not about them. It's about the business, the employees, and the suppliers.

"It's important to forgive people and control your emotions. One thing I learned from Paul is never to attack the person on an issue. Try to understand people, and look at the issue, not the person. That's been hard for me, to keep myself calm and keep emotions out of decisions, but I do try.

"Now if you do the right thing every day, you don't have to worry about your profits, either. Focus on your people, your employees, your customers, and the profits will come. That, I learned from Paul."

The value of self-control and self-discipline, ironically perhaps, spills out far beyond just affecting self. It becomes a way of building bridges to others. When you have the self-control to keep emotions in check, put others first, and learn to listen, you're able to truly value others.

"Paul had a way of controlling the outcome of a discussion," Weaver remembers—but it wasn't by railroading his own way. "He had ways to use logic and to stay focused on the right thing and for everyone to be involved. Sometimes we couldn't get everybody on the same page, but he would keep coming back, making sure, 'Okay, did you understand his answer? Did everyone else understand Paul's answer on that?' We'd end up going around the table and asking questions about an issue. We've had some store managers who will just talk, just keep goin' on and on. You get two or three of those in a meeting, and it will just go on forever! Paul would say, 'Okay, now nobody talks unless you're holding this pen.' It was hard for some of them, cause they want to interrupt you! But you're saying your piece, and then you pass the pen around the table. He had a very good sense of people."

Paul Zurcher's ability to keep his own mouth shut, to lead gently, and to respect others had a profound impact on his life and his business.

"If you followed him and saw him operate, saw him in council meetings, people listened to Paul. He didn't want to control everything. His opinion would come out, but it wouldn't be the first opinion. He wanted to hear everybody's story, or what they were thinking, before he'd come out with his thoughts."

"[Paul] didn't want to control everything. He wanted to hear everybody's story, or what they were thinking, before he'd come out with his thoughts."

Weaver's lifelong partnership with Paul Zurcher also had a profound impact on the Zurcher family. Paul's son, Mark, said, "The respect that Dad had for Paul Weaver was mutual. When we think of respect, integrity, wisdom, and just a really good friend, we think of Paul Weaver. It's not hard to see the good in Paul—it just flows out naturally. We've been fortunate to partner with many great individuals, and Paul is certainly one of the greatest of the great!"

Weaver has similar sentiments. "Partnership with Best-One was the best thing that ever happened to me and to my family. I was only twenty-six at the time, with two kids, in debt up to my ears. I had to go to the bank and borrow more money than I could ever think about. I know I borrowed over a hundred thousand dollars, and the interest rate at the time was probably at twelve or thirteen percent. I had no choice but to make money! With your back to the wall, you'd better! You have to do whatever it takes. I told my wife that—I'm gonna do whatever it takes. If it's fifteen hours a day, seven days a week, that's what it's gonna be to make it go.

"Being part of the Best-One group enabled us to be where we are today. It proves that if you're willing to work hard and do the right thing, you can succeed. I was planning on going into business, back in '72 and '73, and I was looking at an operation in Harrisburg, Illinois. The guys wanted to sell it to me—they were getting up in age and so forth—and I could own a hundred percent of it, but I didn't have the buying price, and I know you gotta have volume, so I chose to become a lesser partner and work with Paul and his group. And it's paid dividends for my family."

Weaver shakes his head. "What gets me is a lot of guys want to be there right now. They don't want to earn their wings, so to speak, they just want it today."

But success in anything comes with discipline, with time, and with good decisions. Maybe profoundly, it also comes with mistakes.

"We made mistakes. We've hired the wrong people, we've opened stores and ended up closing them down, but Paul always told me—I would apologize to him and say, 'I failed here, I should have done this, I should have done that'—and he would always say to me, 'Well, we're doing more right than we're doing wrong. We can expect some failures, but we're doing more right than we're doing wrong, so focus on that, not the ones that you lose money on.'"

The Weavers and Paul Zurcher remained in business together until the very end. Paul Weaver remembers the day he learned of Paul's passing.

"We were headed down the road on business, and Sue called me, because I had asked her to keep me updated on Paul. You know, my wife and I pray a lot when we travel, and I said, 'Let's pray the rosary for Paul.' We were praying and really concentrating on the mysteries of Christ, you know, his sufferings on the cross. We were in Henderson. It's about a twenty-minute prayer. We got to Masonville and we stopped to eat, and I paid my bill and then Jon texted me and said, 'Paul passed.' We had been praying when he passed. It hit me hard when Jon texted—I was really looking forward to talking to Paul again.

"That's what I miss most about Paul: just talking to him, consulting with him. He's still with me. His wisdom is still with me, making me stop sometimes and think about something in a different way. That's what I miss most, but I've been working real hard to always think about every issue, how he would handle it, how he would look at it. He always was, 'Do the right things right.'"

In the real world, "doing the right things right" looks like self-control. The self-control to care. The self-discipline to forgive and to listen. And the intentionality to build a business and a life on caring for others more than gunning for profits. That's the legacy of Paul Zurcher—a legacy that still carries into his business today.

* * *

"The hardest thing about being a leader is leading yourself. A leader leads by example; he is self-disciplined and self-controlled. Leaders model execution and attitude, openness and respect."

— *Paul Zurcher*

In his speeches, Paul liked to share short stories to illustrate a point. He often told one story about two boys and a bird that explains the power of choice—something Paul believed we all have.

"There was a wise man who lived up on top of a mountain. Legend said he could answer any question asked of him.

Two boys hiked up the mountain; they thought they knew how to outsmart this wise man. One of the boys held a small bird behind his back in both hands and asked the wise man, 'Is this bird dead or alive?'

"The man said, 'Son, if I say he is alive, you will crush him in your hands. If I say he is dead, you will open your hands, and he will fly away.'"

Paul wrote about this story, "You see, in your hands is a great, great power: the power of choice. Between any stimulus and response, there is a moment, and in that moment you decide how to act. Do you embrace a challenge, or do you give up an opportunity? Do you act with passion and commitment, or do you crush the bird? Choice is the starting point of everything we do."

This image of a bird has been a recurring theme for Paul's family since his passing. Paul's granddaughter Lindsey marveled that somehow her son Kley, only four years old, came away from Paul's viewing with a little decorative bird. As soon as she saw it, she remembered Grandpa's story about the bird and how we all have a choice in how we respond.

A few months later, Paul's grandson Jon had a startling vision of Paul holding a little bird. Jon writes about the experience, "I was lying in bed with the lights off, tossing and turning as I was thinking about some things that were bothering me. A situation was heavy on my heart.

"In desperation, I prayed, 'Lord, help me! Please God, show me what to do. I need help!'

In an instant, Jon began to see the most lifelike dream he'd ever experienced. "First, I saw the side of Grandpa's face. Like I was standing slightly behind him. Next, I noticed Grandpa's mouth was starting to move, as if he was getting ready to say something. To the right, a young boy was standing, looking up at Grandpa. I could only see the young boy from behind, and I noticed he held his hands behind his back and was making a cup with them. He was leaning slightly forward, as if to better hear what Grandpa was saying. Then I saw inside the boy's hands was a bluebird.

"I heard Grandpa's voice as he was telling this young boy a story, 'The boy asked the man, is it alive or dead?' As he was speaking, I saw the bluebird up close. It was precious and beautiful and gentle. As I watched it, the bird looked fragile and afraid. It started to move inside the boy's hands.

"Grandpa continued his story. 'If I say it is alive, you will crush it and kill it, but if I say it is dead, you will open up your hands and let it go free.'

"For the shortest moment, God gave me a glimpse of the front of the young boy, and I was overwhelmed when I realized the boy was me.

"Grandpa finished the story: 'And the answer is in your hands.'

"I knew I held this precious bluebird, and I could not bear the thought of any harm coming to it. With the boy's hands held open, the bluebird flew away and up into the air. It circled around as if deciding what to do. Then it flew into the clouds—totally free.

"In another instant, I was back in my bedroom, staring into the dark room. My body, which moments earlier had been tight with anger, suddenly felt relaxed with peace. God had answered that prayer. He answered my other prayer as well—I realized God wanted me to love as he does."

Jon and Lindsey's stories testify to the fact that Paul's anecdotes were much more than stories. They profoundly affected his family and continue to resonate with those around him. Like in this story, I believe Paul would tell each one of us the same thing: "The power of choice is in your hands. What will you choose? To crush others or to give life?"

Questions to Ponder

Principle #4: To Be Self-Disciplined and Self-Controlled

1. In Paul's speech he said, "It takes discipline and self-control to focus your life. Only the disciplined get really good at anything." He also said, "It all comes down to two questions—what do you want out of life, and are you willing to pay the price?" Do you know the answer to these questions in your own life? Have you taken the time to define what you really want and what it will take to get there? What is your purpose—and is it worth the effort and intentionality that self-discipline and self-control require?

2. When Paul came back from the service he was challenged to set life goals in five categories: mental, spiritual, physical, family, and financial. Have you set life goals in any or all of these categories? If yes, do your goals need revisiting so you can get back on track? If no, why not start today?

3. For his mental goal, Paul chose to read on average an hour and a half each day. He also spent that time listening to books on tape or motivational speakers. How did this affect Paul's life? Do you have—or are you ready to make—a similar commitment to ongoing education in your life?

4. Jay Kesler and Paul shared the belief that duty leads to joy. "Joy is different than fun. Joy is deeper than fun." Both men believed that God would give joy as they did their duty in life. Do you agree with this assessment? Why or why not?

5. Story after story about Paul highlights his self-control in the area of conflict. He was able to keep his emotions

from getting the best of him, and he took practical steps to make sure he kept people separated from issues. What value might self-control in this area have in your business? In your family? In other areas of your life?

6. Paul Zurcher often handled conflict by "planting seeds" and trusting them to grow. Earlier in the book, Paul quoted Stephen Covey: "Trust is the glue of life. It is the glue that holds organizations, cultures, and relationships together. Ironically it comes from the speed of going slow. With people fast is slow and slow is fast." Paul was able to build trust, see conflicts resolved, and watch ideas spread because he had the self-discipline to wait. What role does patience play in accomplishing your goals and developing effective relationships? Is patience an area where you are strong or weak? How could you strengthen the "muscles" of patience to create new possibilities in your life?

7. Paul's unusual intentionality about life—especially his values—coupled with a close walk with God fueled his ability to remain focused, self-controlled, and caring. Would you say you are an intentional person? In which specific area of your life would you like to become more intentional?

8. Paul Zurcher said, "The hardest thing about being a leader is leading yourself." Do you agree with this statement? Why or why not? Paul went on to describe leadership: "A leader leads by example; he is self-disciplined and self-controlled. Leaders model execution and attitude, openness and respect." If you are in a position of leadership, do you display these qualities? If you are not in an official leadership position, how might developing these qualities make you a leader even without a title or recognition?

Principle #5

To Do the Right Things Right

We've all heard about Pavlov's dog; a stimulus produces a response. But we as humans are different. In that second between stimulus and response, we have a choice.

You can choose to be reactive, or you can choose to be proactive. In that second, you make your choice, and the choice carries consequences. Realizing the power of choice gives you a new outlook on the world.

We all know what the right things are. The hard part is committing to doing them. Character is doing the right thing, day in and day out, even when no one is looking.

There's a story about a carpenter who was getting ready to retire. He had practiced his trade so well over the years that he was the best in the area, and everyone wanted him on their crew. One day a manager came up to him and said, "Before you retire, I'd like you to work on one more house, as a favor to me." The carpenter agreed, but his heart wasn't in it. He took shortcuts, and his workmanship was shoddy. When he finished, the manager came up to him and thanked him for his many years of service. Then he handed the carpenter a key— the key to the house he had just worked on.

You are what you do. Or better said, you are what you commit to and do. What are your goals? Goals that remind you where you're going and infuse your decisions? I have committed to three goals. They are service, leadership, and growth. Service is doing everything in your power to help people reach their highest potential. Personal leadership is what makes things happen. And growth in the long run is the only alternative to decline. These commitments determine my choices and remind me to do the right things right.

— Paul Zurcher, from his 2010 speech,
"Nine Life Commitments"

CHAPTER 5

"The most essential quality for leadership is not perfection, but credibility."

— *Rick Warren*[1]

The driveway out in front of the original gas station in Monroe, Indiana, is a wide, rough slab of concrete. The "skyline" of Monroe rises in the background: silos, the outline of the fire station. It's the kind of place where the summer air is full of dust and the smell of cornhusks, where the sun beats down hard while you work.

For Mark and Larry Zurcher, Paul's two sons, that slab of concrete is layered with memories. It all started there, with a single gas station. What would grow to become one of America's largest independent tire networks began with a man and his family working in Monroe. Betty worked in the office. Colleen helped pump gas. And every Saturday afternoon, Larry and Mark swept that drive with Paul. He paid them with change out of the drawer.

It was hard work and a big job, but Paul required that the drive be clean and neat. He wanted every customer to have a positive experience there. His fifth life principle, "Do the right things right," was on display in every part of the fledgling business.

Asked how Paul lived out his life principles, Mark leans forward and says, "The big thing there is he *knew* them." Most people, after all, don't—few can articulate their principles, much less live them out. "And the second thing is he was committed to them. Many people don't know their own principles to begin with, and those who do aren't committed to them. Those two things alone would put him in a one-in-a-million class. And along with that, he had the capabilities to actually put them to work."

For Paul Zurcher, doing the right things right meant having standards—like keeping a tire store neat and clean. It meant appreciating people, working as a family, and making sure your kids learned the value of hard work. Mark recalls working at Zurcher Tire after he finished college: "I did a little bit of everything. Part of Dad's desire was to have people do everything in the store and to understand work. I pumped a lot of gas, changed a lot of tires, put a lot of tires in racks in the warehouse, washed a lot of lightbulbs." Looking back, Mark reflects that it's that kind of work ethic and humility that gives you the understanding to be a leader.

Similarly, Larry said that as soon as they were old enough, they were helping out at the store. "First Dad started us out by giving us brooms and having us sweep the warehouse. We'd go back in between the rows of tires and do our sweeping. We would also help unload the semis when they would come in. Dad's father, Grandpa Bill, was retired, but he would hang around the station because he loved being there, so Dad would send Grandpa out to watch us. We would roll tires out of the semi and stand on the gate of the semi. We would just drop a tire on another tire and get it to roll straight down. We would see how far we could get the tires to roll by themselves." As the boys grew older, they helped change tires in the bays during their Christmas and summer breaks.

When asked if the boys resented working with their dad, Larry shook his head and responded, "It was exciting . . . we knew we were helping."

What Mark and Larry learned at the tire store, Paul had learned on the farm. His commitment to working hard and even more so, working *right* began on the farm with his parents.

"The whole family worked together as tenant farmers to make ends meet," Paul once recalled. "We had to get up early in the morning to do chores. We'd have breakfast and then walk a mile and a half to the country school. Then in the evening we'd walk back from school. If it was harvest time, we'd go back out and work. Then we'd go in when it got dark and have dinner as a family."

If you visit Best-One headquarters today and ask around, it won't take long before a certain iconic story comes up. It was a blistering hot summer day, and Paul was in his eighties. He came by the warehouse to find a group of guys unloading tires from a semi. He watched for a few minutes, frowned, and then rolled up his sleeves. He must not have thought the guys were working fast enough, so he jumped into the back of the truck and started rolling out tires—faster than anyone else. The younger guys quickly picked up their pace and never forgot the work ethic of their boss.

This was not a one-time occurrence. Jon recalls, "When I started working in the bays, Grandpa would have been in his early eighties, and whenever he was caught up on his phone calls and meetings, he would come out and put on a pair of gloves and carry the used tires out to the pick-up area. It was nothing for him to put on a pair of gloves and help the guys out or go out to sweep off the sidewalks so the store was presentable." Paul could easily have assigned these tasks to an employee, but he intentionally modeled doing the right things right.

Jerry Browning, partner and president of Best-One Knoxville, thought back to when he first began working with Paul. "It might have been at the first group meeting we attended as partners," Jerry recalls. "Paul asked me how it was going and if we were getting the work done. I looked at him and said, 'Absolutely, and we are only working half-days.' He looked at me with such a frown; it scared me for a moment. I said, 'Yeah, half-days, seven to seven.' He liked that much better and started laughing. I didn't joke with him about work much after that!" Though Paul had a sense of humor, he did not find it funny to skimp on a full day's work. He lived with intentionality and tried to make each day count.

* * *

"If you help enough people in life get what they want, they will help you get what you want."

— *Zig Ziglar*[2]

To Paul, doing the right things right often meant the ability to think outside the box. It meant knowing the facts, looking for the best solutions, and being creative. And sometimes, it meant extending grace.

Mark will never forget one winter's night in senior high when he fell asleep watching TV at his girlfriend's house. After a first date at junior prom, he and Vickie had begun dating a lot during their senior year. Both would eventually go to the University of Evansville, where their relationship progressed to marriage. But on this particular night, they were still just teens.

"We woke up around two o'clock and I thought, *Uh-oh*," Mark recalls. He jumped into his sports car and started down the road—fast. In the middle of the night, moonlight lit the roads and barren fields in every direction. He approached a stop sign, but he could see for miles in every direction. There was nothing out there, so he decided not to stop.

Bad decision. As Mark tells it, a police car staking out a nearby corner saw him "flying through there like a jet. I was going fast enough that he couldn't get close enough to turn on his lights until I was almost at Monroe."

Mark pulled over, nervously waiting for a ticket. But the cop said something even more frightening, "Let's go to your house and talk to your dad."

That's how life goes in a small town.

"I would rather have been fighting a rattlesnake at that point in time," Mark says, laughing. "So we go home and he wakes up Dad, and Dad was pretty disgusted. He had that look that he used strategically, that look that everybody knows, and I got the look." He laughs again. "He actually kinda scared the cop."

As Mark waited for the boom to drop, the officer surprisingly came to his defense, explaining that although Mark had been driving *fast,* it wasn't like he couldn't see where he was going. The situation was disastrous enough to ground any high school kid for weeks, but it could have gone worse.

"So you know, Dad sits there and thinks about it and says, 'We'll discuss it tomorrow,' and he thanks the cop. And I think I started learning some lessons there, some significant lessons— you know, you don't react too soon, and you sometimes think about things."

These days, color and charisma are highly valued. The ability to be witty, quick on your feet, fast-acting—our modern society values those qualities. But Mark remembers his father as more even-tempered and careful than quick to speak. He was calm, but not a pushover. Rather, Paul was willing to invest something significant in doing the right things right—*time.*

"He wouldn't run off and do crazy things," Mark remembers. "He was laid-back and careful, and he really cared about the facts. We weren't a fly-by-the-seat-of-your-pants family."

In some ways, Paul characterized his era. Both he and his wife came from a time when people interacted with respect and humility, a time that fostered an environment of conservatism and peace. The contrast with today's values can be stark.

Going back to the speeding story, Mark finishes, "The next day he gave me the choice either to stay within the speed limit for a year or not see Vickie for six months. You know, he was using an out-of-the-box solution that some people would have thought was stupid. Most people would say 'just ground the dumb kid.' But Dad knew me. He knew what he was dealing with. Grounding me wouldn't have done any good. He knew me enough to challenge my honor and try to make it a lesson. I learned a lot there, and I gained a lot of wisdom and respect. I didn't like it at the time, of course! That's a good example of how he would think things through and construct a scenario where you would get the results you needed, you would learn a lesson and have a 'win' from it. To me that's characteristic of how he tried to live. It's a good indicator of who he was."

In business, Paul often pursued win-win scenarios. Rather than only considering his own interests, he would try to find a creative solution that would benefit everyone.

Paul would tell partners, "You and I are in a relationship I value very much. You have your needs and wants, and we have our needs and wants. If your needs and wants are not being met or our needs and wants are not being met, let's sit down, talk about it, and see if we can come up with a win-win solution. Sometimes people go down a course that's a lose-lose road. When that happens, you have to change their thinking. We try to work something out." Though they were often elusive, Paul was notorious for finding the win-wins.

After university Mark came back to work for Best-One, where he's now a manager and partner. "I didn't come back because of an expectation," he says, "I felt somewhat of a calling. I kind of figured all along I would do that. I saw what Dad created and saw that it could be something good to sustain and promote."

Mark smiles as he thinks back to those early years and says of his father, "I think the highest compliment you can pay someone is that you learned from them."

For Paul, the life principle to do the right things right was more than just a personal commitment. He recognized that because of his role in leadership—as a father, business owner, and community member—his personal commitments would affect others profoundly.

"A good leader knows what he stands for," he said in a speech. "Decision making is easy when there is no conflict in your value system. You are the captain of your own ship. You chart the course. You set the sails. You determine your own destination. You may have all of the qualities of a leader, you may experience all the success in the world and make all the money in the world, but if you don't have your priorities straight, you will ultimately become a loser.

"It is not enough to think truth, act truth, and speak truth, although to be able to do these in concert is to succeed in life. To be effective leaders today, we need to consider the impact of our decisions on other people in our lives. When we honestly consider the well-being of others before we decide to profit ourselves, we become truly rich and are on our way to becoming an effective leader."

* * *

"Commitment is what transforms a promise into reality. . . . It is making the time when there is none. Commitment is coming through time after time after time, year after year after year. . . . It is the power to change the face of things."

— *Abraham Lincoln*

In a world often obsessed with success, material things tend to be the measuring stick. Keeping up with the Joneses becomes paramount—certainly more important than some antiquated idea of "right." But that wasn't the way Paul and Betty Zurcher lived. Even as heads of a multimillion-dollar company, they remained in the small ranch-style house in Monroe, Indiana, where they'd raised their family. Remarkably considering his success, Paul lived his entire ninety years within three square miles.

"Mom and Dad maintained a modest lifestyle because they were humble," Mark says. "Both realized money wasn't the key to happiness. If you're humble, by default you're going to maintain a modest lifestyle."

A few years ago, Betty excitedly showed her grandchildren her new stove. A basic four-burner model, it was a definite upgrade from her last one, which had served the family for thirty years. Only two burners on the old stove had worked, and it had been like that for years.

Jon shares a funny story about the dent in Paul's car he refused to fix. "Grandpa was very successful but he wasn't showy about it. He liked to drive Lincoln Town Cars, but he would drive them until they got up to two hundred thousand miles. One day I was driving a skid loader in and out of a building, and it was tight enough that I couldn't turn around inside the building, so I had to back out. Grandpa had come and parked beside the entrance. I didn't have good visibility behind me, and I was going slowly, but Grandpa had parked just as I was backing out.

"It is possible to be very successful and not make a lot of money. It is also possible to make lots of money and be a failure."
— Paul Zurcher

"Needless to say, I didn't see Grandpa's car and backed the skid loader right into the front fender. Grandpa didn't feel like he needed to fix it right away, so he drove around with that for quite a few months, and every time I saw it I just felt awful."

Paul and Betty did not draw their identity from their wealth, so for Paul a dent was just a dent. No matter to him.

Paul's attitudes about money shone through in a presentation he gave with Jon. "It is possible to be very successful and not make a lot of money. It is also possible to make lots of money and be a failure. When it comes to money, remember, it is how we use it that makes a world of difference in our lives and others."

Because Paul and Betty lived modestly, they were able to expand their business without taking on more debt. Larry recounts, "After the first store he had borrowed money for, Dad tried to expand using earnings from the company rather than borrowing. He generally was not heavily leveraged. He would try first to have some retained earnings in the business before he would take it out as dividends. He just wanted to reinvest it back in the business.

"He did not live an extravagant life at all. He just tried to watch expenses as closely as he could, and he would use the earnings the business generated to invest in additional locations."

In this way, Best-One slowly expanded without much debt. They weathered financial storms much better than other tire businesses that expanded rapidly and then faded into bankruptcy.

Paul and Betty also believed the right thing to do with God's abundant provision was to give to others. They faithfully supported their church, Youth for Christ, Swiss Village Retirement Community in Berne, the Boys and Girls Club, Taylor University, missionaries, and many other ministries. Directors of these organizations and others Paul had never met often scheduled meetings with him to outline their dreams and needs. Rather than getting frustrated with this intrusion, Paul graciously listened and often gave sizable donations. He approached his giving strategically, however, and concentrated on a few organizations he felt would capitalize on his investment for God's kingdom. Many of these were local organizations that were making a difference for Christ in his community.

Though Paul and Betty lived modestly and gave generously, they still enjoyed the financial blessings of Paul's business. At Betty's funeral during the writing of this book, a few of the grandchildren reminisced about how they enjoyed shopping with Betty because of her impeccable taste. Granddaughter Maureen laughed and said, "She was my shopping buddy. We went shopping all the time, and she taught me how to window shop." Paul and Betty also enjoyed treating the extended family to a nice restaurant. Paul had a practiced technique of pulling aside the waitress at the beginning of the meal and asking for the bill. Even if others tried to offer at the end of dinner, Paul would just smile because he already had the bill in hand.

Though generally like-minded, Paul and Betty did not always see eye to eye on money matters. Colleen remembers when Betty and a girlfriend had been trying to figure out how to sew with the new suede fabric that was in style. One day Betty told her friend with a mischievous smile that she had figured out how to sew with suede. Her friend asked her what the secret was, and Betty said she had bought a new sewing machine. Paul bristled when he saw her bringing it into the house and chided, "I thought we were going to talk before buying that."

"We did talk about it," Betty said. "If you can buy another tire store, I can buy a sewing machine."

Colleen says her mom used a language she knew Paul would understand. Even though Paul might not have seen the value in a sewing machine, he ultimately trusted Betty's discernment. But these instances were rare, because Betty and Paul both agreed the right thing to do with their money was to use it to serve the Lord. Their shared goals and approach to life enabled them to agree about what the right things were—and to do them right.

Questions to Ponder

Principle #5: To Do the Right Things Right

1. Paul said, "You are what you do. Or better said, you are what you commit to and do. What are your goals?" Aside from morality and ethics, goals are how we discover what "the right things" are for our lives, and they help us define how to do them "right." Paul's goals and life commitments gave him sharp clarity in many areas where others struggle. As his son Mark pointed out, Paul was remarkable in that he both knew his values and goals and was committed to them. Do you know your own goals and values? Can you identify "the right things" in your life? Do a "life audit": Are your habits, actions, and commitments in line with your goals? If not, what can you change to make "doing the right things" possible for you?

2. Paul said, "Growth in the long run is the only alternative to decline." Do you agree? Why or why not?

3. For Paul, work ethic was a major part of "doing the right things right." Creativity, logic, grace, and looking for a win-win were also components of this fifth commitment. To you, what does "doing things right" mean? Do you share Paul's standards and values in this area, or does the phrase summon up other standards and values entirely?

4. When Paul took on menial tasks around the business, like sweeping a drive or rolling tires even in his later years, he intentionally modeled doing the right things right. Is it possible that for him, humility was also part of doing the things right? What value do you see in humility, besides its ability to model for others? How could you cultivate humility in your own life?

5. Modern society tends to value charisma, wit, and fast action. But Mark remembers his father as more even-tempered and careful than quick to speak. He was laid-back, but not a pushover. In some ways, he was typical of his era. Which set of qualities—the modern or the more "old-fashioned"—do you see as more valuable? Why?

6. Mark said of his father, "I think the highest compliment you can pay someone is that you learned from them." Whom have you learned from? What are the most valuable lessons others have taught you? On the other hand, what are you teaching others—through your actions if not through direct words? What kind of legacy will you leave behind?

7. Paul and Betty founded a multi-million dollar organization, yet they lived within three square miles their entire lives, staying in the same small ranch house where they

raised their family. Do you see that kind of modest living as admirable? Why or why not? Paul and Betty didn't place much value on material things. How might this have empowered them to achieve success in various areas of their lives—for example, by keeping them out of debt? Could a more modest lifestyle enable you to achieve more in other areas of your life?

8. Paul and Betty also believed the right thing to do with God's abundant provision was to give to others. They approached their giving strategically, concentrating on a few organizations they felt would capitalize on their investment for God's kingdom locally and elsewhere. Is giving a part of your financial life? Do you see giving as an investment? In what ways could giving "pay off" in your own life, in your community, or in other areas?

PRINCIPLE #6

To Be a Positive, Enthusiastic, and Passionate Person

This principle is easier said than done! Do you ever talk to yourself? What do you say? For example, think about the thoughts that run through your head when you wake up in the morning. How many of those are positive? Or do they go more like, "Gee, it's already six a.m.? I am so tired, but I better get moving. Time to shovel off the driveway again. Well, guess I just better expect a backache. And then at work I've got to meet with that angry client . . . what a bad day this is shaping up to be."

What you put into your mind—your programming—determines the person you will be. Programming creates beliefs, beliefs create attitudes, attitudes create feelings, feelings determine actions, and actions determine results.

Take great care of what enters your mind and what you allow your mind to dwell on. How well you guard your mind is crucial to your relationship with God.

How do you master your mind? By choice. When I first returned home from the service, I made goals in five areas of my life. One of the goals I made was to feed my mind. I made a commitment to spend an hour and a half a day reading, listening to tapes, or talking about ideas with great people.

That commitment has helped me to challenge my programming, develop new beliefs, and change over the years. The commitment, that choice I made, has changed my life. It has allowed me to change my attitude and bring my actions in line with my beliefs.

You know, life is ten percent what happens to us and ninety percent our response. You can change your life if you change your attitude. Choose to be a positive person. Enthusiasm is the spark that transforms being into living. Enthusiasm makes you want to wake up and live! It makes you alive for everyone around you. If you have it, thank God for it. If you don't, get down on your knees and pray for it! The most important choice you make each day is your choice of attitude.

— Paul Zurcher, from his 2010 speech,
"Nine Life Commitments"

CHAPTER 6

"A man will succeed in anything about which he has real enthusiasm."

— *Charles Schwab[1]*

Paul pushed through the revolving doors of the hotel located just next to the Indianapolis airport. Alongside him walked two of his business partners, Don Schneider and Paul Swentzel from S&S Tire. Paul searched the crowded lobby, and his face broke into a smile when he spotted Denny and Darwin Meier, two potential new partners.

The five men shook hands and exchanged pleasantries before taking a seat in a quiet corner. On the table in front of them, Darwin and Denny had laid out their performance and sales projections, estimated gross profits, and a map of targeted sales areas. Clearly Darwin had put his marketing-major skills to use for this presentation.

From the outset, Darwin began talking a mile a minute about their goals and plans for Meier Brothers Tire Supply, Inc. The other men listened and nodded throughout the hour-long presentation. Paul and the other partners asked a few pointed questions, which Darwin answered in great detail, but otherwise they listened in silence.

When Darwin finally finished the presentation, one of the guys said, "Why don't we take a break for a few minutes and then come back to talk this over?"

At that, all the others took the chance to stretch their legs, and Darwin found himself sitting alone with Paul. Paul cracked a smile and looked Darwin straight in the eyes. "You really like the tire business, don't you?"

Surprised at the question, Darwin sat quietly for a moment before answering. Then he said, "Paul, why, yes I do."

Just then the other men returned and Paul announced, "Gentlemen, I think we can put this thing together now."

Years later, Darwin wrote that he realized in this first inter-action that Paul Zurcher cared more about the people he part-nered with and their passion for the business than any fancy business plans or presentations. Passion, enthusiasm, "loving the tire business,"—these mattered.

Darwin assessed correctly. Passion and enthusiasm mat-tered to Paul. In fact, Paul called enthusiasm the "difference maker," what sets individuals who succeed apart from individ-uals who fail. Paul quoted from an unknown source, "Enthu-siasm is something that makes us great, that pulls us out of the mediocre and commonplace, that builds into us *power*. It glows and shines; it lights up our faces. Enthusiasm is the key-note that makes us sing and makes men sing with us."

Paul continued to describe this coveted character trait. "Enthusiasm: the maker of friends, the maker of smiles, the pro-ducer of confidence. It cries to the world, 'I've got what it takes.'"

Depending on your personality, this type of enthusiasm might not come naturally to you, but Paul maintained that you can pray for it and cultivate it. "If we have it, we should thank God for it. If we don't have it, then we should get down on our knees and pray for it." Paul wrote that each day he wanted to be "eager in my response to the future." We don't know what the future might hold, but we can choose to be enthusiastic in our reaction to life.

Taylor University's Jay Kesler also remembers Paul's positivity and enthusiasm for life. "Paul admired and knew Charlie Jones, who went by the moniker Charlie 'Tremendous' Jones. Charlie was on the national board for Youth for Christ, and he was a top-ranked motivational speaker and writer at that time—a big leaguer in that world. His trademark was you would ask him 'How are you doing, Charlie?' and he would say 'Tremendous!' Paul had this 'Fantastic!' word he always used."

That story is told over and over among Paul's family, friends, and associates. "You would ask Paul how he was doing, and he would say, 'Fantastic!'" It's always told with a chuckle. And yet, Paul's determined positivity was magnetic. It's clear, from story after story, that his chosen mindset was a key to his success. And make no mistake: it was a choice.

Kesler, who like Paul grew up during the Depression and World War II, remembers, "My father was a man who lived through the Depression. He was permanently scarred by it. Paul was also deeply affected by the Great Depression and by World War II, but he came out in a healthier place. I think it was the glass-half-full thing, the whole power of positive thinking. Although Paul grew up in incredibly difficult circumstances and personally participated in history's deadliest war, he did not become a casualty to that. And that is a tremendous thing to observe."

Jay pauses and looks around the crowded student eating area, named Zurcher Commons in honor of Paul and Betty. Students sit with their lunches and coffee, talking and laughing. The scene seems to inspire him. "Norman Vincent Peale talked about the power of positive thinking. . . . Paul knew that the power of positive thinking was a real thing. He understood that the genius of Franklin Roosevelt, the genius that brought the whole nation out of a depression, was to look at the future and not say, 'Gosh, ain't it awful.' Paul didn't spend a minute of his time saying 'Gosh ain't it awful.' He always looked at how to solve the problem. You don't worship the problem. So he *knew* that when you asked him, 'How you doing?' and he said, 'Fantastic,' you might have had a lousy day and so might he!" Jay laughs. "But he knew we weren't going to solve anything by having a pity party."

Far from an empty idea, positivity empowers change. This is something Jay Kesler and the Taylor board saw in action repeatedly. Positivity also enables courage, although it doesn't negate good common sense.

"When it came down to just practical business decisions, was this a good idea or a bad idea, Paul understood math." Jay laughs again. "He could do math. Not all preachers do math well, not all philosophers or educators do math well. I wouldn't call Paul a risk-taker. Paul was what you would call a conservative man. The way he dressed, everything. But he wasn't conservative in a stuck-in-the-mud way. If I said, 'This is going to take a step of faith,' Paul wasn't afraid to take that second step, that step of faith. Paul was courageous. You can't build the kind of thing he built, the kind of business he built, without courage."

Jay sums up the effect of Paul's positivity by pointing to his accomplishments. "He could have stayed in Monroe and had a very comfortable life. But he kept growing and adding partners and stretching, because he knew that was how he would build success. I appreciated that. You would have some people who, unless the math all added up, you couldn't move. Paul was always looking for 'Can we do it?,' which is very different."

* * *

"I heard a great metaphor for enthusiasm a while back. Visualize a pot of water sitting on a hot stove. That water grows hotter and hotter, but you don't see anything happening. At 211 degrees, the water is just hot. At 212 degrees, the water boils! Enthusiasm is that extra degree. Enthusiasm can take you out of the ordinary and into the extraordinary. In business, enthusiasm colors everything you do. It pulls you out of the mediocre and gives you the power to make a difference."

— *Paul Zurcher*

Paul lived life enthusiastically and "wide open," as he liked to say. This applied to all aspects of his life—his driving, his tire orders, and his baseball teams. Jim Wertenberger, one of Paul's first business partners, wrote this memory of Paul:

"You may not know that in the early 1960s Paul knew one driving speed—FAST! As his Firestone territory manager, I traveled with him on several truck-tire sales calls. We'd climb in his Oldsmobile, he'd put the pedal to the floor, and I had to hold on tight just to stay in the front seat!"

Paul drove safely even into his nineties, but employees and family members shake their heads and chuckle when they remember the speed at which he did it.

Jim continued, "I also remember once when Paul ordered far more tires than would fit in his three-bay tire store, so we decided to store them in his garage at home. No room for the Oldsmobile to park inside, and what would Betty have thought about all those stinky (you know the smell of fresh rubber) tires at her home? Paul must have tiptoed around the house for weeks."

Larry also recalls Paul storing tires in their garage during his childhood. "Dad only had a small building for his retail store, so all the extra inventory of tires he kept in our garage. There would be stacks of eight or ten tires piled high in our garage. Mark and I used to crawl over the top of the tires and play." He laughs. "We couldn't even get the car in there and had to park it out in the driveway. Those tires were valuable, so that's where we stored them."

Paul's enthusiasm to hit his numbers with the different dealers might have caused some inconvenience for Betty and the kids, but their family also shared Paul's vision of what he wanted to accomplish at the store.

Paul's enthusiasm extended beyond his faith, his family, and his business, to baseball. Paul's daughter-in-law Sue would make a game of tallying up how many baseball references Paul dropped into conversations at a business meeting. "He averaged about five!" she said. "He used phrases like, 'We hit that one out of the park,' 'They are pitching us a curveball,' or 'We have to make sure we are covering all the bases.'"

Paul's nephew, Steve Zurcher, shared another baseball memory of Paul from over forty years ago:

"My father, Vernon Zurcher, was the coach in the Zurcher family, but Uncle Paul also had a great love of sports and was quite a competitor himself. In the mid-seventies, Zurcher Tire sponsored a softball team in the Decatur Industrial League. Bob Hurst was our coach, and Paul wore a #10 Jersey with the name OWNER on it. Approximately two-thirds of the team was comprised of guys who worked full or part-time at Zurcher's. Paul coached third base for our team.

"Paul Zurcher was a true competitor and here are three reasons why. One, I remember how Paul closed the store early when we had a six o'clock game so we could all get to the diamond early for warm-ups! Two, one morning following a particularly bad loss, Paul took Coach Hurst into the back room and wanted to know what in the world was wrong with our team. We were not hitting the ball well at all. Something needed to be done! Three, on the flip side, if we won our game, Paul always treated the entire team to Dairy Queen. If we lost, *no treats!* Needless to say, we worked hard for a victory. We won more than we lost. We were even league champions—at least once. We had great times on the diamond. We loved our owner, and we loved our ice cream!"

Paul summed up his enthusiasm in four statements: "I want to be enthusiastic in my reaction to life. That's dynamic. I want to be eager in my response to the future. That's vision. I want to be excited about my responsibilities to God. That's focus. I want to be energized by my relationship with God. That's passion."

He finished his speech with, "These things will help us become more alive than everybody around us. These things will keep us useful for God until the day we walk before him in his presence. God Almighty, I am yours. Take me and use me and make me a difference maker in the world in which I live."

* * *

"Light yourself on fire with enthusiasm and people will come from miles to watch you burn."

— *Attributed to John Wesley*

Thinking back on adolescence, most people would agree it is a time of change and turmoil. Without a strong guide, it's easy to lose your way. For Maureen, her grandfather was that guide during her teen years. Paul would take her out to dinner at a local restaurant, like Bob Evans. She would talk, and he would truly listen.

Those conversations at Bob Evans and similar places were a lifeline for Maureen. Her parents were going through a divorce, and like any teen, she found it difficult. Paul would take her out regularly just to talk, to ask how she was doing and how she felt. And he would share his own heart and the things he believed, things that could really make a difference in someone's life.

"He would give a lot of Scripture and talk to me about doing things the Christian way," she remembers, "how to handle conflict in a good way. He talked to me about how to honor my parents, how to talk respectfully, be self-controlled. He would always say, 'You reap what you sow,' so it was important for me to stay positive."

As she reflects on other things Grandpa Paul told her, one gets the sense these weren't just platitudes from someone who didn't know the cost. They were the mantras of someone who lived them out every day. "He would always say, 'Fight every battle on your knees.' And another one: 'Just obey God, and leave the consequences to him.'"

There's nothing glamorous about advice like that—pray, trust, do what's right, sow what you want to harvest. They're the kind of down-home, old-fashioned principles best shared at a booth in a diner over a sandwich and a cup of coffee. But they—and the person giving them—can carry a teenage girl through hardship. They can build societies and change lives. It's the kind of personal connection Paul did so well.

Asked what characteristics of her grandfather she would most like to emulate, Maureen responds quickly. "Building people up. There are not enough people who do that. A lot of people just tear other people down. Helping people see what's special about them, just helping them grow . . . it's pretty cool. I want to do that."

She laughs. "I'm not sure Grandpa even *saw* the negative things about people. He saw the good in everyone. He saw what was special about people and called that out. That's why, when someone did something wrong, he would be disappointed. I never saw him get angry, but he would be disappointed with people."

For Paul, one of the most important of these teachings was that of "obeying God and leaving the consequences up to him." That had intensely personal application in relationships: if you were only responsible to do what was right, and not responsible to make anything turn out, then it didn't really matter if others made wrong choices. You could still love them, still respect them, still invest in their lives.

Colleen, Maureen's mother and Paul's daughter, reflects that maybe it was this habit of only seeing the good in people—of focusing on what was special about them—that helped keep Paul so positive all his life. She said about Paul's positive thinking: "How you frame the matter in your mind makes all the difference. If you look at the situation negatively, it will spiral down from there." Paul believed there was no reason to dwell on the negatives, rehash disappointments, or replay situations that had gone badly. God had all that covered.

Even at the end of his life, Paul continued seeing the good in others and mentoring others. Brad Lehman, a family friend and member of Paul's church, shared how Paul served as a father figure for him and a model for life and marriage. Brad patiently waited many years for God to bring him a wife and family. During that desert time, Paul continually encouraged Brad to trust God. When God did bring a wonderful wife and family, Brad first went to Paul to ask his approval before proposing to Sherry. Paul, at the age of eighty-three, gladly served as best man in their wedding.

In a speech, Paul reflected, "Sometimes, life becomes so busy we don't stop to think about how much the influence and help of other people affect us. I want you to stop for a moment, and see if you can answer these questions: Who won the Indy 500 in 1996? Who invented the television? Who was president in 1852? Did anyone get all three questions right? Now, answer these questions: Who was your first boss? Which high school teacher meant the most to you? Which pastor married you? I'll bet you could answer all of these questions!

Paul believed there was no reason to dwell on the negatives, rehash disappointments, or replay situations that had gone badly. God had all that covered.

"Don't other people play a huge role in your life? Be intentional in your relationships—nurture them. You end up where you're going in life because of the choices you've made and the people you've known."

Maureen, now a young adult, chose to enroll at Taylor University—a place very close to Paul's heart. As she goes about her classes and activities, she thinks often of Paul's advice during those difficult times. She remembers that we always have a choice to dwell on the positive, and with this positive attitude, negative circumstances can't control you. Paul liked to say life is ten percent what happens to you and ninety percent what you do with it.

Chances are he told Maureen that too.

Questions to Ponder

Principle #6: To Be a Positive, Enthusiastic, and Passionate Person

1. Paul's speech asks the question, "Do you ever talk to yourself? What do you say?" Have you ever seriously thought about the power of self-talk? How could changing what

you say to yourself—first thing in the morning and as you meet challenges and opportunities throughout the day— change the course of your day? The course of your life? Pay attention this week to the thoughts running through your head. Put effort into being intentional about what you choose to tell yourself.

2. Paul also said, "What you put into your mind—your programming—determines the person you will be. Programming creates beliefs, beliefs create attitudes, attitudes create feelings, feelings determine actions, and actions determine results." Have you ever thought of your programming as something you can control? What "programs" could you create that would make a practical difference in you today?

3. Paul often said, "Life is ten percent what happens to us and ninety percent our response. You can change your life if you change your attitude." Do you agree with this? Why or why not?

4. Why do you think Paul considered a question like "You really like the tire business, don't you?" so important? Why would he base a business decision as pivotal as whether to partner with someone on the answer?

5. Paul called enthusiasm the "difference maker," what sets individuals who succeed apart from individuals who fail. He maintained that no matter your personality, you can pray for enthusiasm and cultivate it. Does enthusiasm come naturally to you? If not, have you ever tried to cultivate it? What were the results?

6. Jay Kesler, who like Paul grew up during the Depression and World War II, contrasted Paul's end results with those of his father, whom he called "permanently scarred." What

factors do you think enabled Paul to rise above the trauma
and scars of war? Do you agree with Jay Kesler that positive
thinking made a big difference?

7. Paul was not only enthusiastic about his faith, his family,
and his business, but he was also passionate about baseball.
What is the place of hobbies and fun in the life of a busy
professional? Do you have hobbies or interests outside of
work? How do they benefit your life? If you don't have one,
can you think of a hobby that would positively impact
your life and the lives of others?

8. Paul maintained we reap what we sow. Is this true? Are you
sowing what you want to harvest?

Principle #7

To Never Compromise My Integrity

What's the most essential quality in a leader? Credibility. In other words, trust. Trust is the bottom line, the single most important factor in human relationships. It is the glue that holds people together. When you gain people's trust, you start to earn their confidence, and that is one of the keys of leadership. Leadership by personal example is one of the most effective forms of leadership.

A man walked into a restaurant with his family. He handed the restaurant owner a wad of one-hundred-dollar bills and said someone must have dropped it outside the restaurant. The owner took the money and told the man he'd try to find the owner. A little later, while the man and his family were having supper, the restaurant owner came by to get his name and address, in case no one claimed the money. He mentioned to the man how surprised he was at his honesty, because no one would have known if the man had just taken the money. The man said, "I would have known. And what's more important," he said, pointing to his family, "they would have known."

That man showed his family they could trust him. He showed leadership by example. If we're going to experience greatness in life, we must have the foresight to see

*our potential, the faith to believe what we see, and the
courage to act on it.*

*What values govern your life? Integrity, caring, and
learning are three foundational values that I aspire to
every day. Integrity is the foundation of character; it is
being faithful in action to your values, your promises,
and your words. Caring is the foundation of everything
we do. Learning is the foundation of growth and is irre-
placeable with the world changing around us. These values describe who we can aspire to be.*

— Paul Zurcher, from his 2010 speech,
"Nine Life Commitments"

CHAPTER 7

"What is good character? Be faithful to your most important core personal values. Be faithful to your promises, be faithful to your word, and be faithful to other people."

— *Paul Zurcher*

The entire Zurcher family, Paul's children, grandchildren, and great-grandchildren, gathered around the long table and ordered breakfast. The kids made all kinds of noise, as kids do, and played under the table and colored on their placemats. The adults, however, were subdued. Paul was leaving for Cleveland the following day to have a serious surgery. Since Paul was in his nineties, the family all quietly wondered whether this would be the last time they shared a meal together.

Lindsey offered a prayer, but nothing seemed out of the ordinary until it was time to leave. Trying to hold back tears, each family member gave Paul a hug before leaving. They were optimistic and prayerful but couldn't help the sinking feeling in their stomachs.

After breakfast, Paul squeezed in one last business meeting before he visited Betty at the nursing home and then left for the hospital.

With such a serious surgery looming, Paul might have excused himself from such a meeting, but he cared deeply about his family and the business. The other family members who were involved in the business met him down at the tire store to hash out a few pressing issues. One had to do with a gray area, common in business, in which a number of solutions to the problem might be justified. They needed to discuss how best to handle an insurance situation.

A number of years earlier, the Best-One stores had created their own independently managed healthcare plan with all the stores contributing to help with the coverage. The plan worked in theory, but a number of large claims in the same year could stress the plan financially. The family knew of such a claim that might be filed soon, and they considered whether to influence the employee to file it with the spouse's insurance company. This decision could mean the difference of hundreds of thousands of dollars for Best-One.

Together, however, Paul and the rest of the family agreed to stick to Paul's seventh principle, "Never compromise my integrity." Even to the tune of hundreds of thousands of dollars, they were not willing to waver on this principle. They would do what they had given their word to do, which was cover everyone under the plan.

"Do you trust me?" Paul asked rhetorically in one of his speeches. "Gaining trust is essentially building another's confidence in me through what I say and do. The most important thing to realize is that it is *your* job to build the trusting relationship. Trust is a two-way street, but it starts with me. Communication never begins with being understood, but begins with understanding the other person. We must keep in mind the importance of dealing honestly, keeping our promises, and living up to our commitments."

In business, murky waters are all around. One of Paul's driving principles, however, was *never* to compromise his integrity.

When Paul said never, he meant never. Even when filing his taxes, Paul didn't try to cut corners, hide profits, or take more exemptions than allowed.

As the head of Best-One accounting, Larry witnessed this firsthand. He shares, "One of the nice things about working for my dad was that once I told him, 'We cannot do this tax-wise,' he did not push it further because he did not want to do something against the law or shady. He would also speak to the point among other business partners, to make sure they knew it was unethical and not an option in his businesses." Paul was not willing to sacrifice his integrity to save a few dollars or even thousands of dollars on a tax return.

"Integrity, for me," Paul said in a speech, "means always trying to do the right thing. It means being faithful in action to our most important core values, to our promise, to our words. You can't be a person of ninety-percent integrity. You either are a person of integrity or you aren't, and your organization will follow your example."

Other murky waters in business include declaring bankruptcy or filing lawsuits against those who have wronged you. It is within a corporation's legal right to apply for bankruptcy protection, even if the principal shareholders have the personal wealth to pay the debts. This did not sit well with Paul, however, and he always chose to pay the bank loans or suppliers personally.

Larry shares how this resulted in long-standing goodwill between Best-One and their suppliers. "Bankruptcy was not an option that he considered. There were some corporations and some partnerships for which, usually due to mismanagement or theft—and there were occasions when there was sizable theft— he had to make some tough calls. Dad was always careful to try to keep his emotions out of it.

"Even though maybe a manager had stolen large amounts of money from him, in his mind, he would still try to think, *I need to treat this person with dignity and respect and love.* If the company was closed and he could have filed for bankruptcy, he never did. He just personally paid the debts that were owed to the banker or suppliers. He did that a number of times when he didn't have to."

Larry adds, "Bridgestone Firestone and the other suppliers remembered that too, so they never were really concerned to extend Paul credit. They knew what he had done for them in the past, so that built trust with the suppliers."

Mark also spoke to this: "Dad never sued anyone or declared bankruptcy. He would work out a solution. It was his nature to offer grace. And he would offer a lot more grace than most people would have offered, without question. He could be very hard when he needed to be, in a constructive sense, but when it came down to offering grace he would always be willing to go the second and third mile. If you're going to err, err on the side of grace."

Maybe the waters of business are not as murky as people believe. Paul knew his guiding principles and knew what the Bible taught. All he had to do then was apply those to all of life, including his business. To never compromise your integrity actually seems quite straightforward when you think of it like that.

* * *

"Duty makes us do things well, but love makes us do them beautifully!"

— Phillips Brooks[1]

A principle like "never compromise my integrity" is put to the test when one seeks to choose the higher road while stuck between a rock and a hard place. The 1978 Firestone tire recall was such a test. Firestone ended up recalling over seven million

Firestone 500 radial tires—the largest tire recall to date. As a primarily Firestone distributor, this put Paul in a tough spot, and he had to choose how to respond.

Larry remembers those trying days. "Firestone stood behind replacing all of those tires, but they pretty much relied on their dealers to take care of the customers and be the contact point. Dad and a lot of the other Firestone dealers were very loyal to the Firestone brand at that time. Back in those days, tire dealers sold one particular brand, which is completely different from now, when most dealers carry all the brands.

"Dad in Monroe, and all the other tire stores, spent a lot of time talking to the customers as they came in, and they always had to watch their attitudes and look at it as an opportunity to build a better relationship rather than look at it as a bother. It would be so easy when a customer came in for the recall to say, 'Well, we're not making a sale, and we're not making a profit on this. It's just a bunch of additional work we have to do.' Dad made sure we looked at it as a chance to serve and establish a long-term customer."

Paul chose to make it right for the customer even if he could have blamed others. He and his employees worked fifteen-hour days to service all the customers with recalled tires. Larry remembers, "There was a short period of time when they were swamped, because everyone wanted to come in right away. They stayed open until the last customer was taken care of." Paul and many of the other Best-One dealers were willing to do whatever it took to care for the customer.

Paul Weaver recalls a similar situation when he had a choice of how to respond. "I remember a guy came in on a Friday evening with two tires that separated. He threw them at my feet, said a few choice words, and went across the street to eat. We were open back then from seven in the morning till eight at night, and then Fridays till nine. I pretty well worked ninety percent of the time—just wanted to be there.

"He came in, and I got tires on his car and he said, 'How much do I owe you?' I said, 'I'm sorry you had problems, you don't owe me anything.' Well, the next day he came back in, and he bought two Firestone deep treads for his tractor and he brought his neighbor with him who bought tires too.

"That's how we grew the business back then. Through word of mouth, just by taking care of the customers, meeting their needs—doing what's right. I would tell the managers, 'You take care of the customers. If they come to me they're gonna get what they're asking for, and you're gonna look bad. I want you to look good. We can always talk about it later, but you take care of the customer.' A tiny percentage of people will take advantage of you, but ninety percent of people will not. They just want what's fair. I believe that had a lot to do with expanding over the years."

Paul Weaver remembers another occasion when a Best-One partnership went south: "A long time ago, we had a fifty-fifty partnership with two other guys, and they were failing in that partnership, and they came to us and said, 'We're gonna go bankrupt.' They had gone out and borrowed money from a bank, and it was in the hundreds of thousands of dollars, and they didn't have board approval—we didn't even know these loans existed.

"We didn't say anything to them, but we were driving back, and Paul [Zurcher] said, 'So what do you think about the bankruptcy?' And I said, 'Well, I don't want bankruptcy on my name. I would rather take the business over, get them out, and pay it off.' I didn't have a lot of money. Paul said, 'Well, I agree with you one hundred percent.'

"So that's what we did. It cost both of us about two hundred fifty thousand dollars, which was a lot of money but we did it, felt good about it, and let those guys off the hook, where they didn't lose a dime. That's the way we handled things. We weren't gonna let something like that on our names. The banker was relieved! He was in trouble because he'd made a mistake lending to those guys, but we were able to tell him, 'No, we're gonna pay you.'"

Over decades in business, Best-One developed a reputation for never leaving anyone in the lurch. Paul never declared bankruptcy, never sued anyone, never left anybody holding the bag. Paul Weaver just laughs. "It gets you into trouble sometimes!"

Though memorable, these weren't the only recalls or hitches in the tire business over seventy years. Nate Zolman shared a story about a recall and his interaction with Paul. As a young man, Nate worked with his father, Bud, at Zolman's Tire & Auto Care.

"My favorite Paul Zurcher story is from February 2001, just after the Firestone Ford Recall. We had our Zolman Tire year-end board meeting in Monroe with Paul, Ray Monteith, Dad, and myself. It was a very positive, upbeat meeting with good results.

"Paul offered to give us a tour of Zurcher's new warehouse, which I believe was a non-heated former lumberyard building. It was about fifteen degrees that day. In perfect pecking order, like ducklings following their mother, we walked down the rows of tires. Paul was in front walking at a blistering pace (as usual), Ray was second, Dad third, and me last.

"With all the recall problems and Wilderness AT issues at that time and all brands on national back-orders, we walked inside this huge, primitive building, and as far as the eye could see were approximately ten thousand NON-recalled Wilderness AT tires stacked on the floor. Row after row after row.

"Ray looked back at Dad and grinned. Dad looked back at me and winked. Then he quickly shook his head, trying to convince me not to open my big mouth, but too late! I cupped my hands around my mouth like a megaphone and yelled very clearly, 'Dad! I know where all our back-orders are!'

"Paul stopped immediately but did not turn around. Ray looked at Dad, concerned for him because of my big mouth. Dad was shaking his head in disgust and giving me that look only a mad father can give.

"We all quickly looked forward to see Paul's reaction to such a blunt comment. Paul was still facing forward. His shoulders were shaking up and down, silently laughing.

"Paul finally turned around and faced us. With a twinkle in his eye he told me, 'I think Jeff can spare a few tires to help you out.' The next day three hundred tires were delivered to Zolman Tire."

Nate wrote about this experience, "I have been blessed for over forty years to have amazing mentors like Paul Zurcher, Ray Monteith, and Bud Zolman. My success would not have been possible without their example and fearless trailblazing."

Paul and these other partners modeled how to conduct their business with integrity and character in good and bad circumstances, through profit and loss. At times integrity did cost— but Paul would say it was worth every penny, both in long-term business and in personal benefits.

* * *

"This story of the Cross is the story of forgiveness and triumph. A story which tells us that no matter how great the wrong, we can be forgiven if we ask God to forgive us and have a forgiving spirit."

— *Paul Zurcher*

Paul gnawed on his lip as he read the invoice again. Five thousand tires. He had promised and sold all the tires weeks ago but still had not received them from Bridgestone Firestone. Every day it seemed a few more customers and dealers called to question when their tires would be delivered as promised. Paul felt like he was running out of explanations.

His musings were interrupted when one of the receptionists called out, "Paul, you've got to come see this."

Paul hustled to the front showroom and looked out the picture-glass window. A caravan of five long semis with "Bridgestone Firestone" emblazoned on the side rolled through the streets of Monroe toward the warehouse. But Paul wasn't expecting his shipment from them for another week or two.

Paul and a few of the salesmen followed the trucks over to the warehouse. With the trucks lining up to unload, one of the drivers jumped out and handed Paul an invoice. "The tires you ordered, Mr. Zurcher."

Paul didn't know how to respond. Two guys from the warehouse opened the truck's back doors, and Paul's jaw dropped. Thousands of Firestone Supremes stood stacked inside. Paul needn't have worried about more explanations and excuses to dealers. He had the tires he had been waiting for.

The man behind that miracle delivery was John Gamauf, president of Consumer Tires, Bridgestone Firestone North America and a man whose history with Paul went a long way back.

John recalls, "I first met Paul in the mid-eighties when I was president of Firestone North America—all products. I've dealt with a lot of dealers—hundreds and hundreds of dealers—but there was a level of respect that was unspoken between Paul and me. He could look at me, and I could look at him, and he treated me like family, and I treated him back the same way. If he told me something, I could take it to the bank, and I treated him back in the same way. I think that was our special connection."

John remembers how the tire delivery happened. "In the early nineties there were many strikes by the United Rubber Workers and they seemed like they were targeting us more than the other tire companies. When they target a company, that means they try to shut you down and the majority of workers leave. Our job is to make sure we have enough tires for our customers during a strike period. We did that for many years, but it wasn't working out well. So we decided to take our most popular tire line, the Supreme, and move all the molds to Japan. We started this one year before the strike so when the strike happened we would be ready.

"Sure enough, we had a strike, and Paul from Monroe placed an order for five thousand tires, and he was told he would get them in about ten days. Ten days came and went and the tires didn't show, so he talked to customer service. What they saw in the computer, they said it should be just a few more days. So Paul said, 'No problem.'

"A few more days go by and nothing happens, so Paul called back again and customer service said, 'I don't know what to tell you, but they say they are on their way.' Someone in Japan was falsifying information that the tires had been shipped, because it takes ten days to ship tires on the water. They go through all these canals to get to the United States, especially for five thousand tires, which is a good-sized order.

"After about two weeks of not getting any answers, Paul called me. I want to tell you, he only called me when he really, really needed something. He wouldn't waste my time for a small thing.

"As soon as my secretary told me he was on the phone, I picked up. I would always say, 'Hey, Paul. How're you doing today?' And he would always say, 'Fantastic!' It was guaranteed that was how he said it. It didn't matter; that was his attitude. He passed that on to me—I was going through cancer at one time, and he would call and ask how I was doing and I would say, 'I'm doing fantastic!'"

This time, of course, Paul had an enormous problem on his hands. Five thousand no-show tires meant a lot of unsatisfied partners and customers, and he was the one ultimately responsible. But he gave the usual answer—"Fantastic!"—and kept his cool.

"Anyway," John continues, "I said, 'What's on your mind?' He started to tell me the story about the five thousand tires. I said, 'Paul, let me get right back to you. I will get right on it.' So I go over to customer service and ask my people to find out what's going on. In a short period of time, I found out someone was falsifying the information, and the tires had still not left Japan.

"You know, this is your largest customer, the customer who is always there for you, so we need to be there for him. I marched up to the twelfth floor where our CEO was and kind of busted into a meeting. I said, 'I have a big problem here. We promised this customer. He's waited all this time, he needs the tires, he has them sold. He needs our help.' They said, 'What do you want to do?'

"I said, 'I'll tell you what I want to do. I want to take the five thousand tires in Tokyo, and put them on a 747, and I want to fly them all the way to Chicago. We will have trailers waiting on the runway. When the plane lands, we'll load those five thousand tires into five semis and we'll drive them right to Monroe, Indiana.'

"They said, 'Oh my gosh, how much is that going to cost?'

"I said, 'I don't care how much it costs, because we need to do this for a customer who has always been there for us.' It pretty much ate up all the profit we made on the tires.

"Paul had found out from customer service that the tires were still in Japan, so he was expecting them in a couple of weeks. Within forty-eight hours, here come five trailer loads of those five thousand Supremes.

"Paul picked up the phone and he called me and he said, 'Uh-uh-uh. Thank you very much. I don't know how you did it, but thank you very much.'"

John didn't feel the need to tell Paul what it took to make it happen. "That again was that unspoken level of respect and trust we had. I called him when I needed help with a product launch, and when he needed that order I put them on an airplane—five thousand tires overnight."

To John, Paul was "the customer who was always there for us." It wasn't a label lightly given. Laughing, John recalls an inside joke that embarrassed Paul but underscored how deeply these men respected and relied on one another.

"Whenever I saw Paul, I would walk over and get down on my knees and kiss his ring, like I was meeting the pope or something. Nobody really knew why I was doing that. Paul knew, and he would get embarrassed. I didn't care if we were at the Indy 500 or in front of hundreds of customers, I would get down on one knee and kiss his ring.

"Here's the story behind that. I had a new product I was launching, a huge product with brand-new technology. I had the factories build hundreds of thousands of these tires. We began to launch the new product, but not everyone understood what it was all about. So unfortunately, it wasn't going well. I was going over to customer service every day asking how our orders were doing, and we were still sitting with a lot—hundreds of thousands—of tires. I thought, *What are we going to do with all this inventory?*

"So I called up Paul, and I said, 'Paul, I need your help.' I told him that we had this great product that nobody really understood and I was on the line for a lot of tires. Do you know what he did? He said, 'I'll get back to you.' Well, he took the next three days to personally call every one of the Best-One members and say, 'I need you to place an order with Bridgestone Firestone today, and here's how many tires I want you to buy.' He called every member in every state Best-One operated in until he got it all.

"About three days later, I walked into customer service and I said, 'How we doing?' They shared with me that the Best-One group had bought over a hundred thousand tires. So you can understand why I got down on my knees and kissed his ring, because he saved my butt! He never said anything else about it. He knew and I knew. I will never forget that."

With Paul's deep emphasis on respect for others and on building effective relationships, integrity was just one more natural piece of his whole worldview. He kept his promises and stood by his partners—even though at times, doing so could hurt.

His grandson Jon recalls a time when a partner had stolen quite a bit of money. "Really Grandpa was loaning money to the business, so he was pretty directly stealing money from Grandpa. They had lost a lot of money, and what we could identify had been stolen, the man agreed to give back. He just didn't want Grandpa to let him go—to fire him. What he stole was a huge amount; you could have bought a house with how much money he stole.

"Grandpa said, 'You know, the trust has been broken. I don't think we can have a business relationship going forward.' Then he called this man by name and continued, 'But you are a child of God and God loves you, and I do too. We are asking that you repay what was taken, and we will part ways. I'm not going to prosecute you. Let's agree to part ways and move on. You've got a family to take care of, and we've got a lot of people in this business and we need this business to succeed.' This person just stole from him, but Grandpa's first response was 'You're a child of God.'"

> *"If [Paul] said something, he would carry through with it, and they could trust what he was saying."*

Larry remembers how Paul valued integrity. "In general, in all his talks with suppliers, you could always count on Dad's word. If he said something, he would carry through with it, and they could trust what he was saying. That's what he said about his favorite suppliers too. Even if there were some tough decisions and things that had to be said, he would always respect them as long as they were honest and straightforward."

Questions to Ponder

Principle #7: To Never Compromise My Integrity

1. In his speech, Paul said, "What's the most essential quality in a leader? Credibility. In other words, trust. Trust is the bottom line, the single most important factor in human relationships." Who do you trust? Who *don't* you trust—and why not? In business and in the rest of your life, identify the top three characteristics or actions that built lasting trust with you. Commit to use those same characteristics or actions to build trust with others.

2. Paul declared, "Leadership by personal example is one of the most effective forms of leadership." At Paul's funeral, his family, friends, and business partners shared story after story about how true this was in Paul's life. He led

by example, and countless lives benefited. Whose example do you follow? Who do you most look up to, and why? If you are not consciously following anyone else's example, is there someone you could adopt as a mentor and make a conscious decision to learn from and emulate them?

3. Paul also said, "If we're going to experience greatness in life, we must have the vision to see our potential, the faith to believe what we see, and the courage to act with conviction." When you look at your potential, what do you see? Do you have faith in it? Are you acting on it with conviction?

4. "Paul knew his guiding principles and knew what the Bible taught. All he had to do then was apply those to all of life—including his business." For Paul, values were the key thing that governed life. He identified his own core values as integrity, caring, and learning. What are your core values? If you do not have them written down, write them down today, and add a few sentences to describe what each one means to you. Aim to write down at least three.

5. Paul defined "good character" as being faithful: "Be faithful to your promises, be faithful to your word, and be faithful to other people." What does faithfulness mean to you? What is the role of words—promises, spoken intentions, and other spoken words—in faithfulness?

6. Do you agree that "to never compromise your integrity actually seems quite straightforward" when you know your values? Why or why not?

7. Over decades in business, Best-One developed a reputation for never leaving anyone in the lurch. Paul never declared bankruptcy, never sued anyone, never left anybody holding the bag. What is your reaction to that? Do you consider

this an admirable track record, worth emulating? In your opinion, do the pros of such a stance outweigh the cons—not necessarily in number, but in value?

8. Paul Zurcher and John Gamauf formed a relationship based on trust and respect. Name two ways personal integrity affects relationships—both in business and in the rest of life. Have you ever considered how making the "tough calls" integrity demands may set up better possibilities in the future through the power of relationship?

Principle #8

To Plan for Tomorrow Today

As Rick Warren said, "There is nothing quite as potent as a focused life; one lived on purpose."[1] Throughout history, the men and women who have had the greatest impact are the most focused, the ones who mix their passion for their goals with foresight and planning. Take the apostle Paul. He was responsible for the spread of Christianity throughout the Christian empire because of his single-minded focus on sharing the salvation that is Jesus Christ.

Informed passion is passion with a handle on reality. When your vision is fueled by informed passion, it is unstoppable, always in focus, immune to distraction, and never in doubt.

But your informed passion will go nowhere unless it comes from your relationship with God. Each new direction will be a false start unless you are open to God's guidance in your life. Aligning yourself with God's will starts when you give yourself over to Jesus—when you praise him as your Savior and trust him to forgive your sins. But really aligning yourself with God is a long, never-ending process. As you grow in your faith, as you test other influences against the Bible, you become in awe of how perfect God's plan is: a plan that includes each one of us. We learn to develop confidence that, as we head in God's direction, we are going the right way and he will be there to encourage and empower us.

Remember what God told the prophet Jeremiah? "'For I know the plans I have for you,' declares the Lord, 'plans to prosper you and not to harm you, plans to give you hope and a future'" (Jeremiah 29:11). God is with you, every day, guiding you. You just have to trust in him. The best place to start is through prayer.

— Paul Zurcher, from his 2010 speech,
"Nine Life Commitments"

CHAPTER 8

"An idea is worth a dollar—a plan, well executed, is worth a million."

— *Paul Zurcher*

Nine a.m. on a Saturday morning—too early to be sitting in a business conference, even with a dynamic speaker like Paul Zurcher. The college students gathered in the classroom slumped over their desks.

Paul, at the age of eighty, strode to the front of the room and held up a crisp one-hundred-dollar bill. "We will be giving away a few of these during the presentation," Paul said and smiled. "Make sure to pay attention so you can answer the questions at the end." He was offering a small fortune to the college students. At least twenty-five students bolted upright in their chairs.

Paul turned to his grandson and daughter-in-law. "Jon and Sue, what do you say we tell these folks what it's like to build a family business?"

For the next hour, the three Zurchers interwove anecdotes and favorite quotes into a presentation for budding business students. Paul not only had the business knowledge to share but also the credibility of building a successful family business from nothing.

At one point, Paul discussed the advantages of Best-One's organizational model, an unusual configuration of partnerships oftentimes with ownership given to the store managers. Paul said, "Some advantages to a small business are that you can be your own boss. You can implement creative solutions. You are independent. In our organization, we try to combine those advantages with the market strength of a larger organization, but relationships are what drive the whole thing."

Sue compared these partnerships to the covenantal relationships in the Bible. Both parties commit to the relationship wholeheartedly—a bond not easily formed and not easily broken.

Later on, Sue wrote about these partnerships, "Paul's business structure was different from the norm. This reflected who Paul was and how he treated others. Paul's business grew by partnering with other tire dealers in their businesses. This allowed the partner the freedom to continue managing his own company in the manner that partner desired, while being able to draw on the expertise and strength of the group. Paul's partners truly had full control of the destiny of their individual businesses.

"The key to making this work was Paul's devotion to his partners. The partnership superficially looked like a business contract. But with Paul, it was so much more. It was more like a covenant. When Paul entered into a partnership with another tire dealer, Paul became akin to a family member. He gave a hundred percent of his knowledge, expertise, and time to that partner. He was there for the tough issues as well as the easy times, and this extended not just to business issues, but also to personal. Paul selflessly shared in his partners' joys and griefs on a personal level. From weddings to deaths in the partner's family, Paul was there. When sudden hardships came about, Paul would not wait for the partner to call him. He would reach out to the partner. Paul had an uncanny memory for details, and he used this to remember his partners' families and personal issues. He was a mentor as much as he was an astute business partner."

At the end of his college presentation, true to his word, Paul quizzed the students and handed out a few hundred dollars. Word quickly spread among the students, and the next two sessions were packed. The students, however, came not only for the prize money but also to hear a man filled with passion for his business.

The organization of Best-One is not a traditional business model, and it can be complicated to understand. Jon explains, "We really aren't structured like a lot of other corporations or organizations. Grandpa started out of a one-bay tire store and grew it and then eventually had the opportunity to buy into another store. What makes us different from a lot of other businesses is, a lot of other businesses when they grow become very top-down, and everything comes from the top.

"When Grandpa has partnered with people, his model has been to help people achieve their dreams. He would meet people in the tire business, maybe salesmen or managers or maybe tire service people. Grandpa would work with them—somebody who had a dream of being in business and had potential. He would back them and help them get started. He would help finance the business. They would run the business on a day-to-day basis, and then they would partner together."

Jon continued, "In this partnership, Grandpa brought the operational knowledge, the purchasing power (as the business grew he was able to buy so much deeper), and he also brought the relationships with other people in the industry. He brought sound business sense too, and then the partner would bring the leadership for that location. The partner would manage day-to-day operations, create the team, sell the product, and service the customer. The partner would deliver outstanding service at that location.

"So this happened once and it happened again and again. As the business grew, instead of being top-down, it was almost bottom-up, like a grassroots operation. As we were opening new locations in one city and the next, one of the strengths was that at first the stores weren't called Best-One. They took on the manager's name, so like Wertenberger Tire was started by Jim Wertenberger; it wasn't Zurcher Tire. Whenever a partner had their name on the business, they took care of that business in a whole different manner. By giving them that ownership, they really took it to heart and took care of the customer.

"Grandpa had a gift for empowering people. So much of the success of the location—you know Grandpa would give them all the tools—but the success of the location depended on the partners." Jon leans back in his office chair and looks at the ceiling. "It's been a great recipe for success."

In a speech, Paul posed the following three questions to his audience to sum up the driving force behind his business model: his belief in the power of personal choice.

1. How many of you honestly believe, and are totally convinced that if you tried, there is something you can specifically do in the next two weeks that would make your personal life, your family, and your professional life better? Raise your hand.

2. How many believe that the choice is yours? Raise your hand.

3. How many believe that every choice has an end result? Raise your hand.

"Let me tell you," Paul concluded, "whether you realize it or not, what you have just said. You agreed that regardless of how bad or good the past year has been, regardless of how bad or good your present is, there is something that you can specifically do now to make your future either better or worse—and—*the choice is yours!*

"If you have dreams, if you have set goals, if you think about tomorrow, if you work hard and smart, if you strive for lasting quality, if you care about people . . . you have the power within you to reach the stars."

Best-One continued to grow on the foundation of partner relationships. "As Grandpa helped partners get started," Jon explains, "they in turn helped other guys get started. Managers have paid it forward, and there have been chains where this has been done four or five times.

A complicated structure such as this has disadvantages as well as advantages. "The disadvantages are that sometimes we can't make changes as quickly as a top-down organization. Somebody at the top can say tomorrow we are all doing this, and everyone does it. For our organization, it has to make sense for every single store. Stores ultimately are responsible to the shareholders of that store and their board of directors.

Jon once heard Donnie Smith, the CEO of Tyson Foods, speak at a conference and describe the common top-down structure generally seen in a large organization. "It's like a giant pyramid," Jon explains. "You have the CEO at the top, over the other executive officers, and then vice presidents and the assistant vice presidents. Then you have directors and managers, and then you have the people at the bottom of the pyramid, who everyone else sits on top of, who do all the work.

"At this point, Donnie painted a perfect example of what Grandpa created, but I had never heard it said this way. He said,

'At Tyson Foods, we don't have a pyramid organizational chart; we have a peach tree organizational chart. Our senior people, like the presidents and officers, are like the roots and the trunk of the tree. Then the vice presidents and managers are like the branches, and our people who are packaging the food, delivering the food, and interacting with customers are the peaches.' And he said, 'With a peach tree, we want the peaches to steal the show. Our job as the leadership is to make sure we are supplying all of the nutrients and water and everything the peaches need, so the peaches can grow as plump and juicy as possible.'"

Best-One's model *is* complicated, and on the surface it may even look haphazard. But it's built with great intention according to a plan chosen because it was most beneficial to everyone involved. Paul Zurcher's dream, after all, wasn't to be the boss. Paul Zurcher's dream was to make others' dreams come true.

Messy it may be, but like a peach tree, it has a beauty, life, and symmetry all its own.

"In a lot of ways," Jon continued, "that was how Grandpa saw himself and our family with Best-One. Grandpa never wanted to steal the show. He wanted our partners, and their people, and the people at the front counter, to steal the show. Grandpa wanted to make sure, being his humble self, that they had everything they needed so they could succeed to their fullest potential."

* * *

Paul's favorite ten two-letter words: "If it is to be, it is up to me!"

As Paul approached ninety, he had decades of success to look back on—but no life is without trouble. Betty, his beloved wife and partner in every respect, now suffered from Alzheimer's.

The principle of planning for tomorrow today, which had served him through the expansion of his business into the largest of its kind in the nation, became more personal as the end of life approached.

Sitting outside on the patio, Mary Reyling rocks back and forth in a rocking chair. The sun is shining, the birds are singing in the woods, and the kids are playing on the backyard play set. When asked how she got to know the Zurcher family, she starts at the beginning.

Her daughter was a childhood friend of Jackie, Larry's daughter, and Mary was in the choir with Sue. That's how it all really began—at choir. Mary had mentioned to Sue she was interested in a total career change and was considering something like working in hospice. This struck a chord with Sue, because Betty's Alzheimer's was becoming more pronounced and she needed more care. Sue explained the situation but told Mary she would need to meet Paul before anything was decided.

"You kinda know it was God inspired, because we set it all up in church!" Mary says, chuckling. "I wanted to make a good impression. I wanted him to like me and, you know, to be professional. I even bought a new outfit, and I went in there, and I honestly could have come in jeans. He didn't see anything on the outside; he just looked straight into my eyes and asked me a little about myself and what I had done. What I had done was nothing related to that, other than caring for my grandmother when she was ill. He just, with his eyes, he could just tell. And I thought, *He knows me, and I don't even have to say anything.* I had my resume and all the proper things, and he finally turned to me and said, 'Well, when can you start?'

"I knew at that time I was blessed to get this job, because he was so different from any other employer I'd had. He made it easy to talk to him, and I immediately felt comfortable."

Paul and Mary read the same books about Alzheimer's and would compare notes. They determined to keep a very consistent routine for Betty. "For Betty everything was so organized; she was his main priority," Mary says. Paul's primary goal for Betty's care was that she maintain her dignity. Mary and Paul met every Friday to discuss how to help Betty, but they tried to meet and talk without her feeling demeaned.

"The one thing Paul didn't want to take away from her was her dignity—her feeling that she was in charge, so that's basically how I took care of her. She was the one in charge though I was the one guiding it, but I helped make it seem like it was her idea. And Paul was always there in the background, just making sure we had anything we needed."

Paul never lost sight of that goal. "We wanted her to feel needed and respected. He was constantly aware that she still needed that even until that final weekend when she had to go into the nursing home and really until he passed."

Paul followed his eighth life principle as he planned for Betty's care with Mary as well as for her future care in the local nursing home, Swiss Village. On Fridays, Paul would come up with a list of ideas for Betty and Mary to do, like shop for certain items they needed or bake cookies for the employees at the store.

Mary smiles. "We loved making those cookies! I would measure stuff and then set the bowl in front of her. She would just make it perfectly every time. I can't copy it! Her mixing and making each individual one exactly the same.

"Then we got to take them in, and of course we always went into the store first, and I don't know who was more proud, Paul or Betty. We would come in with those two plates and knew exactly how many we needed to make for all the departments. Betty would go walking in, and she would carry the cookies so they knew they came from her. I knew Paul really liked that; I think she had done it in the past, and he wanted to keep it going.

"Tuesdays we would go to visit my mom, Fridays were her hair appointment and nails." Mary and Betty enjoyed shopping for Christmas and birthday presents as well as sewing for the family. And Betty worked regularly alongside Mary at St. Vincent De Paul, a secondhand shop in Decatur operated by a local church. Mary says, "Betty was such an organizer, and she kept the toy section just so neat. Paul was very much for us helping there. He never shied away from having her there. Some people might be embarrassed. Everyone there treated her with the utmost respect, and I was never far from her. And I think that kept her active."

Even at this time in Paul and Betty's lives, Mary was able to glimpse how they had functioned as a dynamic couple. Once, Mary and her mother toured Zurcher Tire. "When I brought my mom down to Zurcher's to see the whole operation, Betty stood tall. Paul did the talking and explaining, but I think Betty grew two inches that day. She was very much aware that she was part of this. I got a glimpse that they were a force together in a very, very good way, that they worked well together, and they had a partnership. They were a power couple together. The pride and the joy and the love they had for each other, you could see all the time."

Paul became the caretaker for his wife, yet Betty still wanted to support Paul as she had for sixty years. "Sometimes," Mary says, "she was insistent that she had to get back to make dinner or get to the store to wait for Paul. She was very concerned; the concern between both of them was always there—the whole time. He was caring for her, but in her mind, she was still caring for Paul."

Mary continues to think back on her time with Paul and Betty. "She was very, very important to him. To this day, I feel honored to have been given what I think was his most prized possession—his wife. Taking care of his wife in those final years while she could still be out and about and could visit her grandchildren and great-grandchildren, getting her ready for Jackie's wedding and for the family photos. The good days far outweighed the bad days. And even then the bad days weren't that bad. I truly loved both of them. I really did. I had great respect when I first met Paul, but as time went on the respect grew and the love grew."

Mary helped keep Betty's mind and body active for two and a half years. "There does come a point when they have to go in," Mary says. "Paul was well organized, and he had it all set up. The transition was really smooth. I was very thankful for how Paul handled it."

Paul had been instrumental in the strategic growth of Swiss Village and knew many of the staff personally. Even though he wanted to keep Betty home as long as possible, he had everything in place for Betty to move there when she needed it. Paul communicated these plans to Mary and the family. "I think it came faster than he wanted it to. That was it. I think it surprised everyone that weekend she needed more care."

The nurses at Swiss Village marveled at how long Betty had been able to remain at home with her advanced Alzheimer's. Mary credits Paul's intentionality and caring spirit for this. "I firmly believe if you are quiet and caring, which Paul exemplified, it keeps it calm. The chaos of a busy lifestyle really upsets people with this disease."

When Betty went into the nursing home, Mary says, "I lost my best friend, my shopping buddy, even if it was only to the grocery store. We were connected at the hip for two and a half years."

Mary's support for Paul and Betty, however, did not end. She offered to continue washing Paul's clothes, picking up the house, and buying some of his food. Paul was delighted, because this gave him the freedom to continue working and also spend as much time as possible with Betty.

Altogether, five years passed from the time Mary met Paul until he died. "When he unexpectedly passed," she says, "it was like losing a father again. There doesn't go a day or two that I don't think of them. It's a cherished memory that will never go away." Like so many during his life, Mary had been touched by Paul's kindness and generosity. He continued to touch those he met even in the last few years of his life.

The same care and commitment he demonstrated in the later years of his marriage was evident throughout Paul's life. Like so many things, it didn't get there by accident. He was intentional from the start.

In an interview with his grandson, Paul stated that the key to keep from becoming overwhelmed in his position was balance. He listed six specific areas of life that needed to be kept in balance for life to work:

1. Keep God first. Apart from him all your relationships will fail.

2. Realize each aspect of your life means completion, not competition.

3. Have the heart of a servant in all you do.

4. Forgiveness paves the way.

5. Blessing your enemies pays incredible dividends.

6. Choose to honor and value people, and their feelings, opinions, time, concerns, and commitments.

In a speech, Paul said, "Commitment goes beyond thinking and dreaming. In all my years in business, I've seen a definite pattern in the way commitment works. It is not instantaneous. You don't develop it immediately. Even when you think you have it, you don't. I have observed that people go through three stages. The lying stage—Deep down you are not certain that you can do it, but you won't admit that to anyone, not even yourself. Next you go through the quitting stage. You go for months and months and work hard and pay a fantastic price. Then things go wrong and you say 'I'm sick and tired of this, I've had it.' But you hang in there and now you make the final commitment, the one that really counts. Now you are on your way to make things happen. This is called *burning all the bridges*."

> "*The best example I know about commitment involves a man who walked on this earth nearly two thousand years ago, a man called Jesus Christ.*"
> — *Paul Zurcher*

For Paul, to plan for tomorrow today meant defining his values, his commitments, and his vision, and then pushing through—in marriage, in business, in relationship with God and others—all the way through to the point of burning bridges.

As in everything else, his greatest strength for tomorrow came from his relationship with God today.

"The best example I know about commitment," he said in another speech, "involves a man who walked on this earth nearly two thousand years ago, a man called Jesus Christ. He was a man who never gave up. He was a man who never quit. He was a man who believed that the impossible could be done. He was a man who believed that all mankind could live together in peace and brotherhood. He was a man who gave everything he had: physically, mentally, spiritually. He is the greatest inspiration I know in life."

* * *

"Strategic thinking is like showering, you have to keep doing it."

— *Olan Hendrix*[2]

Even in his eighties, Paul showed no sign of slowing down, but he also was not in denial that this life would end. He had the assurance of where he would go when he died. As his end neared, one of Paul's main concerns was for his family and his Best-One partners. He wanted to be intentional in his estate planning so that Best-One could continue to grow and thrive.

With his knowledge of accounting and tax law, Larry speaks to the difficulty of the task that faced Paul: "Dad was always thinking of the future. He would set aside a time every year to sit down and talk with Mark and me about how he was preparing, like how much in life insurance he needed to buy to pay estate taxes.

"The estate taxes were what Dad really had to worry about, because when he passed away, we had to go out and get evaluations of every single company by a professional evaluator. You add all those up, and that determines what the taxable estate is. Everything over five million dollars is taxed at fifty percent, and it reaches fifty percent pretty fast. So pretty much fifty percent of all your assets, you have to pay in taxes. It's a sizable tax. Unless you want to sell half of the company, you have to have another source to pay all those estate taxes."

Larry also expounds on the challenges of passing on a company—especially a company as complex as Best-One. "You have to pay the government for the transfer of a family business to begin with, and then you also have the management side of it too. You have to have the people in place who can handle the responsibilities to keep the work going well. Paul prepared for that too, as far as talking about the roles and responsibilities each of us would have. And it's hard to do that without making guarantees, but he never really made promises. He said that every position would have to be earned."

Larry goes on to outline some of the strategies one can use to pay estate taxes: life insurance, gifting, and selling stock. He explains, "One strategy is to buy life insurance, but you have to buy a lot. Another way is to make gifts or transfers while you are still alive, so Dad did a considerable amount of gifting while he was still alive because there's a small amount you can give each year, like right now it is fourteen thousand dollars per year per person. He tried to always give the maximum amount you could give without paying taxes during the year. Then he tried to transfer other stocks during the year.

"In addition to transferring or giving, you can also make sales. So Dad did make some sales of stock to Mark and me. You'd have to get the stock appraised, and then he would sell it and usually take back a note. Then we would turn around and pay him on the note until the note was paid off, but at least when he sold that stock it would be out of his estate. Then any future earnings or appreciation would not be included in the estate."

Not everyone is eager to give up their stock when they are still active in the business; that involves giving up ownership and control as well as future capital. "The hard thing is if you sell it you don't have it anymore, but he cared enough about planning for the future that he was willing to make gifts and transfer stocks while he was still alive. So he had transferred a substantial amount before he passed away. He was willing to do that to save estate taxes and to keep the company going for everyone. That was really what he was concerned about—keeping it going—more so than keeping the stock himself. It was a way of sharing really."

This helped accomplish Paul's long-term vision, which was to continue the success of Best-One. Larry adds, "He definitely planned ahead as far as the day he wouldn't be here anymore. He had the finances in place to keep things going, and he wanted to see that happen."

When asked about the partners' feelings during the transition, Larry believes few were concerned about the estate taxes or really understood how much planning needed to take place for that. More were concerned about who would take up leadership of the company.

"They might have been more worried about the management of it. It wasn't so much the detail management work, because they knew we all could do the details, but I guess it was more the relationships—where you attract new people to the business, people who want to partner with us. Because of Dad's reputation, people wanted to partner with him. Now it's continuing to build that reputation and knowing who can solve problems as they come up or differences in opinion. Even as others want to sell and retire, how are they going to be taken care of? There was a lot of concern from other partners, but more along the lines of who is really going to be the leader."

Mark and Larry intentionally addressed these concerns in conversations with partners and at the annual Best-One seminar. For the first seminar after Paul passed, the theme was "Unite the Fight!" with the idea of honoring Paul and drawing ranks to continue building Best-One. Larry also remembers how Paul included them in partner meetings and conversations for years before he died to pave the way for this transition. These relationships became the springboard for the next generation of Best-One partners. It was all part of Paul's plan.

"All of us are facing the future," Paul said in one of his speeches. "We can [choose to] face that future with a positive, understanding, dedicated attitude. 'Well, you may ask, 'How do I know what that is?' I am about to make a suggestion or two. In the book of 1 Kings is this terrific statement. If you could weigh it, it would be worth its weight in gold. Here it is: 'I will give you a wise and discerning heart' (1 Kings 3:12). That is the promise of Almighty God to every one of us. How are we using it? What are we putting into it?

"These three pounds of tissue called the brain can take you through anything, around anything, or help you live through anything and achieve success and victory.

"Life is really great and wonderful. Life is living each day to the fullest, happiest, and most successful. Don't put off living, loving, giving, and appreciating. Life is too short to be little. Be big, be happy, be enthusiastic, and especially be thankful and grateful! Expect the very best out of life today, and you'll receive blessings and rewards beyond your fondest dreams. You'll appreciate and love life, you'll find goodness and greatness in everyone you meet, and most importantly, you'll like and love and prosper the person you are."

A little later in the speech, Paul said, "There is a definite relationship between what a person believes in his heart and what a person is able to accomplish with his life. However, even though we are capable of accomplishing great things, no human being can meet the challenges of life by themselves. So in closing, I challenge you to meet the Happiness Giver. Take charge of your life. Live your future with a positive, dedicated attitude.

Make the commitment to give life your best shot, and you will have joy unspeakable and a terrific time living."

Questions to Ponder

Principle #8: To Plan for Tomorrow Today

1. Paul said, "Throughout history, the men and women who have had the greatest impact are the most focused, the ones who mix their passion for their goals with foresight and planning." Paul Zurcher's own life is an example of this, from his humble beginnings to following an outline on a napkin to building a nationwide business and caring for his family. Name some other people, in history or in your own life, whose lives illustrate the power of purpose.

2. Do you agree with Paul's assertion that "your informed passion will go nowhere unless it comes from your relationship with God"? Why or why not?

3. One of Paul's favorite Scriptures was "'For I know the plans I have for you,' declares the Lord, 'plans to prosper you and not to harm you, plans to give you hope and a future'" (Jeremiah 29:11). These words were spoken by God to his chosen people in the Old Testament of the Bible. How does faith in a God of good plans affect our own ability to plan—or even to hope? What gives you confidence to plan for the future and hope for good things to come?

4. Paul said, "An idea is worth a dollar—a plan, well executed, is worth a million." Best-One Tire is a good example of this, as hundreds of small partnerships, following Paul's leadership, together became the largest tire distributor in the United States. What ideas are you excited about? Have

your ideas given rise to plans? What plans can you spell out today?

5. Paul saw some of the advantages of small business, which he tried to retain in the Best-One business model, as including the ability to be one's own boss, to implement creative solutions, and to be independent. At the same time, he also said, "relationships are what drive the whole thing." How can the interplay of independence and relationship create a strong business model? How could these two things, held in balance, enrich other aspects of your life?

6. Paul's plan for Best-One Tire was not really to become the boss. As his grandson Jon said, "His model has been to help people achieve their dreams." What is the importance of dreaming to success? Do you choose your own partners on the basis of their dreams? How can you help others achieve their dreams?

7. Jon Zurcher said that "as the business grew, instead of being top-down, it was almost bottom-up, like a grassroots operation." Although Best-One has a clear structure, in some ways it was discovered more than planned ahead of time. How can the value of planning ahead intersect with the values of being open, curious, and exploring?

8. Estate taxes posed a significant challenge for Paul, and he saw the need to make a plan and execute it without delay. He began planning, seeking counsel, and acting on his plan years before his death. What areas of your life need a plan sooner rather than later? What can you see on the near—or distant—horizon that would be better met proactively, rather than waiting for it to come to you?

9. Death is the one event we can't prevent—but few of us really plan for it. Does the story of how Paul planned for

his wife, his family, and his business in his last years inspire you to think about your own final days? What do you need to do? How do you need to prepare? What legacy do you want to leave?

Principle #9

To Live Life Now, and Live It Wide Open

There is a very special Bible verse that encourages us to live and live with passion. It is John 10:10—"I have come that they may have life, and have it to the full." Let's look at this piece by piece. "I have come that they may have life." Jesus came to give us life. But that's not all; look at the second part of the verse, "and have it to the full." God gives us not only life, but abundant life, a surplus of life, a SUPERabundance of life. Our lives, this superabundance of life and love, are all from God. You can have a great life with God's help!

This verse is a source of hope and inspiration. It comforts us in dark times and gives us strength to follow God's path for us. Turn to God's word when you are weary, when you are lonely, when you doubt, and you will find comfort. You can do all things through God who strengthens you. And everything you do—do it wholeheartedly. Every day know how much God has blessed you and gives you a special mission to make a difference in other people's lives.

That is an opportunity to get excited about!

— Paul Zurcher, from his 2010 speech,
"Nine Life Commitments"

CHAPTER 9

"Remember what you are at age eighty-five, you have started to become at age twenty, age thirty, and age forty. How you think about life, how you think about the gift of life, the life God has given you, will determine how you live the rest of your days."

— *Paul Zurcher*

It was a Saturday afternoon in Monroe. Paul, well into his eighties, had a business lunch to attend. The couple he planned to meet with were much younger than he—hard workers looking for an opportunity. They met at The Brick House, a small corner restaurant in Monroe—one of the *only* restaurants in Monroe.

Dave and Sheila Mitchell were about to become leading Best-One partners, as well as personal friends.

Dave reflects on that lunch. "I'll never forget the first time we shared a meal together, when Paul began to ask God's guidance—I mean, he blessed the food, but when he was asking for God's direction on that particular meeting, it had a huge impact on me. It was just so heartfelt. I knew right then I was at the right place for the right reason."

Paul's faith was never secondary in his life. He was a businessman, but he was a businessman who lived his faith like he lived the rest of life—wide open.

That Saturday lunch meeting encapsulated not only his faith but also his commitment to people, his eye for opportunity, and his ability to quite literally change lives. Dave says, "You know, he put us in business. If it wasn't for Paul Zurcher, I wouldn't be sitting in the seat that I am today. I will always be in debt to him. He literally changed our lives, my whole family's life, by giving us such a great opportunity."

At that meeting, they didn't talk much about the tire business. "We talked a lot about our faith and how the Lord had blessed our families. There was a like-minded approach to life. That was what really resonated with Paul in me."

The two men established a special bond. They were kindred spirits, both in business and in life.

Sheila too remembers the impact of meeting Paul for the first time. "This was the first time we'd really experienced someone of faith in business. Usually you have businesspeople and you have faith-based people, but Paul was really the first who was both. It was so refreshing to see that aspect and that approach to everything. We thought that was how you should be able to do it, but we never saw it in action, being done successfully, until we met Paul."

Sometime in the course of that meeting, Paul quoted Romans 8:28, "And we know that in all things God works for the good of those who love him, who have been called according to his purpose," and Dave almost finished the Scripture for him. They knew then this was going to be a special relationship.

After that, Paul brought up his idea. The young couple were looking for an opportunity to get into business but had no idea what that would look like. They had no real means or connections to start out big.

"We were looking for an opportunity," Dave remembers, "but we had no clue where we would end up. We had looked at a lot of places. But when we met Paul, we knew this was something we wanted to be part of: the character, the integrity, the faith. But we didn't know what we were going to do, how we were going to get started with this wonderful company. Would we start in a garage, what would we do?"

The Mitchells would have been happy to take any opportunity. But Paul was thinking *bigger*. He'd been talking to an established tire company and knew they were having some internal struggles and needed someone to take them over. The company had been in business for seventy years. In the Mitchells, Paul saw a solution.

"When this unique opportunity came up, we really didn't have the means, nor did we plan on starting at that level. Paul gave us such a tremendous opportunity. He was so giving and generous with his time and knowledge, his finances, his resources."

Paul put the deal together, and the Mitchells were catapulted into business. They packed up and moved to Lima, Ohio, to take over the company in partnership with Paul.

"We lived the first six months in a hotel," Dave says. "The first year was a little challenging, but it was nothing short of miraculous for us. Paul was so encouraging."

His wife laughs. "Those first six months we had a board meeting every week because the business was in such disarray. It was a trying time—exciting, but trying."

Through the transition, Paul stood by their side. "Paul always made time for me," Dave says. "He took a lot of time for us, and we asked for a lot of his time, and man, it was always very, very special. Paul had a unique ability to make you feel like you were the only person on the planet. To be totally present with you, focused on your needs and your relationship in the moment. He had a remarkable gift for that.

"Paul had a profound impact on me personally. When I would go to spend the day with Paul Zurcher, I would come back—I mean, he just had a unique ability to make you want to be better. Not just in business, but I mean, when you came back from time with Paul you wanted to be a better person. A better father, a better businessman, a better leader. He had a unique ability to bring out the best in people."

* * *

"Dream big—if you're big enough for your dreams, they're not big enough for you!"

— *Paul Zurcher*

Sitting in the office of their Lima location, Dave and Sheila give each other knowing smiles as they swap stories about Paul. Throughout the interview, one occasionally tears up thinking of the impact Paul had on their lives, and the other has to fill in the rest of the story.

"Paul shared with me one time that he felt God had placed him on earth and in the position he was in to help others," Dave says. "It wasn't just words, he really believed that. He lived his life to fulfill what he felt God had called him to do. Some do that through pastoring, and some do that through missionary work. There's a lot of ways to fulfill your call. Paul just happened to do that through tires. He impacted so many people in so many ways, and then you look at their families, and the number is just huge, the impact he had on families and different organizations, and they have impacted others. It was Paul's purpose on this earth, and he felt that, and I tell you what, I think he fulfilled that one hundred percent, and his reward, I think he received it."

Paul told a story in one of his speeches about the misconceptions that often accompany success—and the real price that must be paid. "One person said to me, 'Paul, don't you know it's easy to get excited about something glamorous like you're doing. If you had this lousy job of mine, you wouldn't talk like that.'

"'Hogwash!' I replied. 'I want to let you in on a secret. Work, wherever you find it, implies one kind of thing: detail, monotony, preparation, striving, and weariness. That's what we all have to overcome, no matter what our work is. The first law of leadership tells me to get excited about the job I have right now, even though it may be an unpleasant job. If I act excited about an unpleasant job, it's going to be tremendous if it ever gets pleasant!'"

Paul's commitment to his Nine Life Principles meant that he always continued to grow as an individual—which meant he had a lot to give to others as well. Thinking back, Dave Mitchell says, "I was at a Bridgestone Firestone Tire meeting with Paul when he was eighty-eight years old, and he was there taking notes. We're thinking, Paul, you could teach everybody in here. But he's in there trying to learn, and to get everything he can out of it. And I think Paul wanted to learn, but I think sometimes it was just good stewardship. He wanted to be an example: *Hey, you can always learn something, never stop learning, never stop striving to be better.* Sometimes I think he did it just for that reason."

Sheila adds, "When we left that one session that day, he said, 'It's a good day today; I learned something new.' And I thought, *Wow.* Now every meeting we go to, Dave and I go to every single session. He was so studious: such an avid reader and an avid learner. That was refreshing for us."

Paul's granddaughter Jackie also commented on this characteristic of Paul. "With Grandpa, there was no hidden agenda. He openly wanted to understand. It takes a humble person to admit you don't know everything, and a confident person to constantly learn and improve." Jackie and Paul often could be found huddled in a corner at a family gathering. Though a leader in his own company, Paul found Jackie's work in the banking world fascinating and tried to soak up as much information as he could. Jackie remembers, "He would provide his undivided attention, ask questions to understand, and share experiences. I was always especially in awe of his balance between humbleness and confidence."

"We had some of our best times with Paul by our side," Dave says, "and we would rejoice together; and we had some of our toughest times with him. I learned so much from how he handled those situations. He was always able to find the win-win. One of his lessons to me was, 'Always separate the person from the action, deal with the action, and treat the person with dignity and respect.' Paul just had a gift for that. He truly treated people very, very well, with dignity, love, respect. Paul could be tough and make tough decisions, but I think Paul could scold you, and you walked out of there feeling good about it. He had a unique ability to do that. I saw that a few times in our time with Paul, that he dealt with tough situations and handled it so graciously that we walked out of there just amazed at the outcome."

Sheila nods. "I can remember we were at a meeting in Monroe, dealing with a devastating situation, and I remember the prayer that Paul prayed before we had our meeting was very calming. We realized God's here; he's going to guide us through this situation. I looked at Paul and said, 'What are we going to do?' And he said, 'We're going to separate the person from the action. We're going to deal with the action today.' He was a tough leader; he could make those tough decisions and those tough calls when he had to, but he always did it with grace.

"I remember telling Dave on the way home, 'I can't believe that just worked out the way it did. That was a miracle, what we just saw.' It worked out well for the organization, and it was a truly amazing thing to watch how things could work out when you just trust the Lord. Trust him to guide, govern your life by those principles that Paul governed his life by. God never fails."

"Obey God, leave all the consequences to him," Dave says, repeating one of Paul's favorite quotes from Charles Stanley. "I have heard him quote that time and time again. He mentioned that that day. What a tremendous leader and individual he was."

"He was always a grateful spirit," Sheila adds. "He was always good at giving credit where credit was due. Overall, he was just such a positive person—he would light up the room. Just the way he would speak to you, and his appreciative spirit." She's quiet for a moment. "It's been a tough year without him."

Dave echoes the thought. "I tell you, we truly loved him. We were blessed to be a part of his life and have him be a part of ours. My only regret with Paul Zurcher was I only had six years with him in business. I wish I could have got started with him at a much earlier, younger age. It would have been nice to have had more time with him."

Paul Zurcher lived his life wide open: to opportunities, to moments, to people, to God. Life, after all, is a gift.

"Tomorrow morning when you arise," he said in a speech, "walk over to your window, throw open the window, lean out over the sill, gaze into the beautiful sky, and thank God for the opportunity of work." Paul would have said the same about any opportunity that lies before us, be it for education, for relationship, for growth. "Then go about [that opportunity] with enthusiasm and gusto. Learn to get excited about it. Enthusiasm is contagious. Help spread it."

Just before the interview closes, Sheila and Dave recall one last story. "We'll never forget Paul's face one day on a trip for one of those meetings where he was taking notes, and we came out and met Sue and Betty. And they had just been parasailing. I never forgot the look on his face. Like he was saying, *I never dreamed they would go parasailing! I thought they were going for a walk on the beach!*"

* * *

"Don't put off living, loving, giving, and appreciating. Life is too short to be little. Be BIG, be happy, be enthusiastic, and especially be thankful and grateful!"

— *Paul Zurcher*

Colleen, Mark, and Larry sat solemnly before the funeral director, faced with the daunting task of planning their dad's funeral. The director began the meeting. "I am very sorry for your great loss. Paul was such a wonderful man, and he will be missed by many people in this community." Tears filled Colleen's eyes, and Mark and Larry somberly nodded. He then started to outline what they would need to discuss. Suddenly, he stopped and asked, "Do your mom and dad have a burial plot?"

The three children looked quizzically at one another. Surely Dad at age ninety had picked out a plot in the local Berne cemetery. After a few quick calls, however, they realized he had not. This news led to a hasty trip out to the cemetery and more paperwork to secure a resting place for Paul and someday, Betty.

Looking back on this seeming oversight, Colleen chuckles. "Dad wasn't planning for death; he was planning for life. That's why he wasn't worried about a burial plot. He was still buying tire stores until the day he died."

Many who knew of Paul wondered why he kept plugging away until the end and never retired. With financial success and two sons in the business, Paul could have retired in his seventies and lived a life of leisure. In response to these often spoken and unspoken questions, Paul enjoyed pointing out that retirement is not mentioned anywhere in the Bible. The local senior magazine actually wrote an article that focused on Paul's decision to continue working. In it Paul was quoted as saying, "I thought if I enjoyed what I was doing, I should keep my mind and body busy. Besides, there is no reference in the Bible telling people to retire."

Paul often held up the example of Caleb in the Bible as a man who lived a full life. He was Paul's role model. When Caleb was about to go into battle at the age of eighty-five, he had this to say: "Now then, just as the Lord promised, he has kept me alive for forty-five years since the time he said this to Moses, while Israel moved about in the wilderness. So here I am today, eighty-five years old! I am still as strong today as the day Moses sent me out; I'm just as vigorous to go out to battle now as I was then" (Joshua 14:10–11).

Paul pointed out that Caleb did not retain his strength because he led an easy life. He went through a desert, disappointments, and the death of all his friends. However, Paul said, "Caleb did what no one else in his generation did. He was committed to the assignment, he was excited about the responsibility God had given to him, and he carried it out."

When giving a speech about Caleb, Paul asked, "How many people do you know who at a certain age plan their life so that their life is over?" Then he answers his own question. "My friends, I do not find anything in the Word of God where we are given permission to do that. God gives us life, and it is a wonderful treasure, and I hope that each of you are setting standards in your own life now that say, 'I am going to live for God and live life wide open until the end.' That is exactly the way that Caleb was, that's the way I want to be, and that's the life I want to live."

"What are you passionate about today? [Caleb] never used his age to take the easy way."

— Paul Zurcher

As he often did, Paul shared a humorous short story that illustrated his point. He said, "I ran across this while preparing for today: 'Since I have retired from life's competition, each day is filled with complete repetition. I get up each morning and dust off my wits, go pick up the paper and read the obits. If my name is not there, I know I'm not dead, so I get a good breakfast and I go back to bed.' That's the way that a lot of people live."

Paul considered how people adopt this attitude at the end of their lives. He suggested this attitude actually begins much earlier in life. "I don't know what happens to us, as we get older, but somewhere along the way we begin to quit looking into the future with vision and planning for God to do great things in our lives. It starts before we get old. I see it in the lives of people I know who are very young. They lose the sense of commitment and the excitement they started their careers with."

In the closing of his speech, Paul didn't allow for any excuses. "Why does this happen to people? They have lost their enthusiasm for life, they have lost their sense of vision, and they have lost their eagerness to make a difference. This leaves them with little energy and passion."

Then he asked a pointed question. "What are you passionate about today? I promise you that lack of spirit and passion does not describe Caleb. He never used his age to take the easy way."

Paul could share this speech with sincerity, because his convicting words matched his actions. Even as he aged physically, he still lived passionately every day and touched many lives.

Mark reflected on why his father never retired. "Core to the success of Best-One is that Dad was about helping other people be successful. It would have been disheartening for him not to follow his passion. Life is a journey, and I think that's the way Dad was. It's not events that mark your life; it's a journey, always working toward the end. Getting there is part of life."

On the journey, Paul lived wide open by helping others to succeed and treating them with honor. "Partners were very important to Dad, and they had a lot of respect for him," Mark says.

Paul was perhaps so good at his business that he just couldn't bear to stop. You hear of financial tycoons who die just wanting to earn one more dollar, but money didn't drive Paul to continue working into his nineties. If he could have put it into words, he might have said he wanted to help just one more person—to help make their dreams come true. I believe he accomplished his goal of following the example of Caleb as well. He stayed strong and, with excitement, completed the mission God set before him.

Questions to Ponder

Principle #9: To Live Life Now, and Live It Wide Open

1. Paul's speech declares, "God gives us not only life, but abundant life, a surplus of life, a SUPERabundance of life. Our lives, this superabundance of life and love, are all from God. You can have a great life with God's help!" Do you feel you are living a great life? Why or why not? Does "superabundance" describe your life, or do you feel

something is lacking? Could relationship with God be the key Paul Zurcher believed it was? If so, what would be your next best step toward closer intimacy with God?

2. Paul offered this perspective on our days: "Every day know how much God has blessed you and given you a special mission to make a difference in other people's lives. That is an opportunity to get excited about!" Have you counted your blessings recently? Are you excited about your mission today? How can you make a difference? Sometimes we just need to be reminded that we *are* blessed and that we *can* make a difference in order to walk with gratitude and purpose.

3. Paul said, "Remember what you are at age eighty-five, you have started to become at age twenty, age thirty, and age forty. How you think about life, how you think about the gift of life, the life God has given you, will determine how you live the rest of your days." Whatever age you are, what have you started to become? How has who you are today grown out of who you were in the past? The future is in your hands—today, you are making the person you will be in the decades ahead. What changes could you make—in action or perspective—that would direct your future in a more positive way?

4. Dave Mitchell remembers Paul's "unique ability to make you feel like you were the only person on the planet. To be totally present with you, focused on your needs and your relationship in the moment." How does the ability to focus on other people create a "life wide open"? How might a closed mind or inability to focus make our lives feel more closed in or narrow?

5. Remembering a conversation with Paul, Dave said, "There's a lot of ways to fulfill your [God-given] call. Paul just happened to do that through tires." Have you ever thought of the "call of God" as directly related to your work, your passions, and your everyday relationships? Many of us relegate ideas of God's call to the foreign mission field or church work. What in your life is the equivalent of Paul's tires? Perhaps you're already doing something—that thing only you can do—through your work or family life that fulfills God's call, but hadn't fully considered its value to God and the world. If you are unclear about your calling, plan a time now to pray and also seek out wise friends or family members who can help you identify it.

6. Paul said, "Life, after all, is a gift," which sums up much of the message of this book. This attitude inspires us to live with gratitude and joy. Spend some time thinking about the idea of your life as a gift. How does this change your perspective today?

7. Why do you think Paul never bought a burial plot? This was an uncharacteristic oversight. Do you agree with Colleen's assessment that he "wasn't planning for death; he was planning for life"?

8. What do you think of Paul's decision never to retire? Do you see retirement as positive or negative? Do you see it as a cessation of work, or as an opportunity to do different or better things? What does your view of retirement say about your view of work? Of your job? Of your future?

9. Paul asked this pointed question of his audience: "What are you passionate about today?" How would you answer that question?

CLOSING SCENES

"Obey God and leave all the consequences to him."

— *Charles F. Stanley[1]*

Before Paul opened his eyes on Good Friday of 2015, he felt a deep throb of pain pulse through his body. Swinging his legs over the side of the bed, he struggled to stand and walk to the bathroom. He reached for a bedside table, but his hands grabbed nothing as his legs gave out. He collapsed on the floor.

A few hours later, Paul gasped and opened his eyes. *I must have passed out,* he thought. His arms shaking, he pulled himself along the bed to the phone. He called Zurcher Tire and told his two sons, Larry and Mark, "Boys, I need help. I must have fallen. I'm too weak to get up."

Within five minutes Larry, Mark, and Jon burst into the house. Paul had been prepared to give a sermon at the Swiss Village Retirement Community that very day—a special sermon, unlike any other message he'd given. He had worked on it for months, convinced God was giving it to him to share.

But instead, he was rushed off to the hospital.

* * *

In the coming days, tests revealed tumors that were suspected to be cancerous. When the doctors confirmed the tumors were malignant, Paul elected to have surgery to remove the cancer. He hoped this would extend his life expectancy by a number of years. He had often talked about win-win solutions, and this was one for him. If the surgery was successful, he would continue to serve the Lord; if not, he would enter into his Lord's presence. Many of his family members also suspected Paul was willing to go through such a painful surgery because he wanted to continue caring for Betty as her Alzheimer's advanced.

No matter the outcome, Paul was prepared. Larry remembers how, before the surgery, his father had his Bible out: "He was preparing himself. He would close his eyes, and you could tell he was praying. He was not scared of dying at all. We asked him if he was scared. He said, 'No, I'm not at all nervous. I'm ready.'"

Paul lived through the surgery but never returned home after suffering congestive heart failure during his recovery.

In the hospital, Paul wondered aloud why God had not allowed him to give his sermon for the Good Friday service. Paul had spent a number of months preparing for it and had felt the Lord guiding him in a distinct direction.

The reason became perfectly clear on the day of Paul's funeral. To a packed sanctuary, Paul's pastor preached the exact sermon Paul had planned to give. The topic—one he had never before spoken about specifically—was obedience.

Though he hadn't known it, Paul had been writing his own eulogy. In it he encouraged his audience, "Obedience to God creates a firm foundation for living the Christian life. Those who obey out of love for Jesus build a solid life for themselves of strength and endurance. Terrible storms may hit them, but they can never destroy them."

Paul had planned to quote one of Charles Stanley's 30 Life Principles, "Obey God and leave the consequences to him."[2] They were the exact words Paul said in the hospital when he learned he had cancer. And they were the words that would encourage his friends and family at his funeral: continue to obey God and leave the rest up to him.

Paul's life had come full circle. When he was a young boy, his father told him, "Paul, whatever you do in life, always obey God fully. If he tells you to run your head through a brick wall, go forward, expecting him to make a hole." Now, even as he entered his eternal home, Paul encouraged those left behind with the same message.

Paul Zurcher's life was a gift—a gift to him, a gift to his family, a gift to his business partners, and a gift to everyone he met. It was a gift given by a good God and lived in friendship with him. Paul was not a minister or a missionary. Like he said, he "served God by selling tires." He didn't preach at people, but everyone knew about his faith. He lived it.

Appendix

The Miracle of Obedience

Sermon Prepared for 2015 Good Friday Service
Read as Part of Paul's Eulogy

If I were to pick two things in life that made everything different for me, the first, and it was the greatest single experience I ever had, was finding Jesus Christ and committing myself to him. And the second thing was that I learned to pray. These two things revolutionized my life. What a pity that so many human beings never find Christ and never learn to pray! They miss the greatest things in this life. This is what Jesus has been saying to us through the years. Really astute people make this discovery: Christ can change your life. Prayer and obedience can change your life.

Take Hold of Life

Luke 20:38 says, "He is not the God of the dead, but of the living, for to him all are alive." This verse speaks of a God of life who has a power that can lift us above ourselves—that can give us a great grasp of life and victory over all our weaknesses; that can throw back our fears and fill our minds with the courage of fire to live with power. And only a few people reach for it. The others are content with something ordinary—something halfway alive. But we were never meant to be this way. A human being is carefully constructed and is meant to be a tremendous person.

One way to start becoming such a person is just to say, "By the grace and power of the Lord Jesus Christ, I'm going to find interest in life; I'm going to put interest into my living. By the grace and power of the Lord Jesus Christ, I'm going to live with delight and excitement; I'm going to live with enthusiasm."

There are some very simple but life-changing principles that I glean from the verses in Matthew 26:36–46. If you were to develop three lifetime principles from this passage of Scripture, what would your three principles be?

Fight All Your Battles on Your Knees

As I focus on Christ's experience in the garden of Gethsemane, my first lifetime principle would be, "Fight all your battles on your knees and you'll win every time." The most powerful thing you can do, the most awesome privilege you have in this life, is to talk to the heavenly Father about anything in your heart. Fight all your battles on your knees and you'll win every time.

What does it mean to fight our battles on our knees?

Simply this—that you and I lay our petitions before the Lord. We must spend time in his presence, listening for his answer.

Why should we fight our battles on our knees?

1. **It is the biblical pattern.** Throughout Scripture, we see God's servants falling on their faces before the Lord.

2. **When we turn to the Lord, we are no longer battling on our own.** No one can help you more than the Sovereign of the universe (Psalm 103:19). He acts on behalf of those who trust in him (Isaiah 40:31).

3. **Prayer connects us with the Holy Spirit and his power.** If you have trusted Christ as your personal Savior, the Holy Spirit dwells within you. We can accomplish nothing for God apart from the Spirit's power.

What can you expect if you fight your battles on your knees?

You can expect not only comfort, assurance, and encouragement, but a new focus. The enemy wants us to dwell on our problems, like how we can defend ourselves or get revenge. Victory, however, is found in turning our eyes to God. He operates on behalf of those who are willing to trust and obey him.

The disciples often saw Jesus off by himself in prayer. Seeing the power, wisdom, and joy in his life, they asked him to teach them to pray as he did. They wanted to connect with God in an intimate relationship and experience his awesome presence.

Are our lives characterized by our time before the throne of grace? Do we inspire others to communicate with and listen to the Lord? Believers who turn their struggles over to the Lord have supernatural peace even when their circumstances don't change (Philippians 4:6–7).

How can you fight your battles on your knees?

1. **Set aside time to be alone with God.** Find a quiet place and devote yourself to the One most capable of helping you. Choose a definite time to spend with the Lord in prayer, a place where you can be alone with him, and make the commitment to pray daily.

2. **Listen quietly.** The Lord desires to have an intimate relationship with each one of his children, but you will never know him better unless you take the time to listen for his voice.

3. **Expect him to bring up other issues in your life.** He may want you to deal with rebellion, unforgiveness, or bitterness in your heart. Until you repent and surrender to the Lord, sin will keep you from experiencing God's best and enjoying a close relationship with him.

4. **Remember that in a battle there can only be one general.** Freely express your desires, but don't expect God to take orders from you. As you surrender to his guidance, he will engage his supernatural power on your behalf.

5. **Know that battles are God's tools.** Some put their trust in themselves and pursue relationships, accomplishments, or possessions instead of a relationship with the Father. The Lord has taught me to see all adversity as allowed by him. This truth will protect you from bitterness toward those who wrong you. Romans 8:28 says, "And we know that in all things God works for the good of those who love him, who have been called according to his purpose." In a battle, you and I may lose money, pride, or control over a situation, but if the struggle brings us to the point of total surrender to the Lord, we will always win spiritually.

Obey God and Leave All the Consequences to Him

Again as I focus on the life of Christ in the garden, my second lifetime principle would be "Obey God and leave all the consequences to him." I draw this principle from Charles Stanley's *30 Life Principles,* which I have spent a great deal of time reading and studying.

What a difference it would make in our lives if we lived by this principle! Scripture says, "Everyone who hears these words of mine and puts them into practice is like a wise man who built his house on the rock" (Matthew 7:24). Obedience to God creates a firm foundation for living the Christian life. Those who obey out of love for Jesus build a solid life for themselves of strength and endurance. Terrible storms may hit them, but they can never destroy them.

As we apply the following principles to our lives, we will begin to obey God with confidence and joy, knowing he can be fully trusted to keep all his promises.

1. **Trust God with your life and all that concerns you.** There is no way to go wrong if you place your hope and trust in God. He created you, and he loves you with an eternal love. Therefore, he will always lead you in the very best way possible. Wait on the Lord for an answer to your problem or situation. When in doubt, refuse to move ahead unless you know that God is leading you.

2. **Meditate on God's Word.** When you saturate your mind with the Word of God, you gain his viewpoint. When a temptation comes, you will know right from wrong and can act accordingly.

3. **Listen to the Holy Spirit.** God continues to speak to his people today. He speaks to us through his Word, the Holy Spirit, and through the words of a pastor or trusted Christian friend. We become sensitive to the Spirit of God by spending time with him, praying, and studying the principles in Scripture.

4. **Be willing to wait or walk away when the way before you is unclear.** If you desire to please God above all others, obedience to him will require you remain firm. If you do not sense clear guidance in your situation, ask God to confirm his will to you in his Word. He will

never contradict Scripture. His will for your life always lines up perfectly with what the Bible says.

5. **Leave the consequences to God.** Obedience may not be easy; you may receive criticism from others or face fierce obstacles and opposition, but it will always put you in a favorable position before God. He will take care of all that concerns you; therefore, stay on the path of obedience and leave the rest to him.

Obedience Always Brings Blessing

My third lifetime principle would be "Obedience always brings blessing." God promises to bless joyful obedience. We delight his heart when we choose to rely on the power of the Holy Spirit to do what he commands us to do.

When you choose to obey the Lord, he will bless you. This is because obedience always leads to blessing. I have always told people who say they do not understand why God is asking them to do a certain thing that, if they will obey him, he will reward them with a sense of peace and joy that compares to nothing this world has to offer. Therefore, set a goal to obey the Lord and watch him work in your life. Those who know the greatness and goodness of God and those who seek to identify fully with Christ's life have a great passion to obey God.

Our heavenly Father places a high value on obedience. He prefers it even to sacrifice or the outward expression of worship (1 Samuel 15:22). In fact, our obedience is the ultimate expression of worship and service (Proverbs 21:3).

Mature Christians express their desire to obey God in three general ways:

1. **A Passion to Know the Bible.** To know what God requires of us, we must know what he has commanded. God's commandments have not changed through the

ages, nor have they been altered according to culture, custom, or technological advances. God's Word is absolute and enduring (Psalms 119:15–16; 105; 106; 143:10).

2. **A Passion to Live in Righteousness.** Very simply, living in righteousness is doing what is right before the Lord. It means gladly keeping his commandments and statutes. It is turning away from sin and toward his statutes. It is turning away from sin and toward what is holy and acceptable to God (Psalms 97:10–12; Proverbs 11:30; 12:12, 13; Romans 2:7–10).

3. **A Passion to Receive Daily Direction from the Lord.** To have a heart for obedience is to have a deep desire to receive daily direction from the Holy Spirit. To obey is to walk in his ways, step by step, trusting that God is leading you and that he will correct you should you make an error. We must observe what God is doing around us and daily ask him, "What is your will, Lord?" (Psalms 25:4, 5; 141:8–10; Jeremiah 42:1–6).

Ultimately, these three desires work together. The more we explore God's Word, the greater our understanding of righteousness and how the Holy Spirit works in us to do God's will. The more we trust the Holy Spirit, the more he reminds us of God's Word and leads us into righteousness. The more we desire to be right before the Father, the more we will want to read his Word and listen for his voice.

I would like to close with this verse: "We will serve the Lord our God and obey him" (Joshua 24:24). What a motto for success! When we make the Lord our own, choose to serve him, open our hearts to his work, and obey him, our own Promised Land opens wide before us, and we receive all the blessings he's planned for us to enjoy.

END NOTES

Preface

Charles Jones, *Life is Tremendous* (Wheaton, IL: Tyndale, 1968), 85.

Introduction

Rick Warren, *The Purpose-Driven Life: What on Earth Am I Here For?* (Grand Rapids, MI: Zondervan, 2002), 180.

Ibid., 32.

Principle #1: To seek God's friendship, fellowship, and guidance

Heartsill Wilson, *A New Day*, originally titled *A Salesman's Prayer* (1954).

Principle #2: To develop effective relationships

Jim Collins, *Good to Great: Why Some Companies Make the Leap . . . And Others Don't* (New York: HarperBusiness, 2001), 13.

Principle #3: To treat everyone with honor, love, dignity, and respect

Stephen R. Covey, *The Eighth Habit: From Effectiveness to Greatness* (New York: Free Press, 2004), 162.

Principle #4: To be self-disciplined and self-controlled

Eric Hoffer, *Reflections on the Human Condition* (Titusville, NJ: Hopewell, 2006), 26.

Jones, *Life Is Tremendous*, 98.

Leo Tolstoy, "Three Methods of Reform" in *Pamphlets: Translated from the Russian* (Christchurch, Hants., Free Age Press, 1900), as translated by Aylmer Maude, 29.

Principle #5: To do the right things right

Warren, *The Purpose-Driven Life*, 277.

Zig Ziglar, *See You at the Top* (Gretna, LA: Pelican Publishing, 1986), 2.

Principle #6: To be a positive, enthusiastic, and passionate person

Charles Schwab, *Succeeding with What You Have* (Mechanicsburg, PA: Executive Books, 2005), 23.

Principle #7: To never compromise my integrity

Phillips Brooks, as quoted in Elizabeth Peabody, *Primary Education* (1916), 190.

Principle #8: To plan for tomorrow today

Warren, *The Purpose-Driven Life*, 32.

Olan Hendrix, as quoted in John C. Maxwell, *How Successful People Think* (New York: Center Street, 2009), 57.

Closing Scenes

Charles F. Stanley, *The Charles F. Stanley Life Principles Bible* (Nashville, TN: Thomas Nelson, 2009), 90.

Ibid., 90.

Appendix

Stanley, *The Charles F. Stanley Life Principles Bible*, 380.

Ibid., 90.

Paul's parents –Mr. and Mrs.
William Zurcher

Young Paul

Paul with his first
car – a 1941 Chevy

Paul in the Army

One of many tires Paul worked on

Paul & Betty young and in love

Paul & Betty's wedding picture

Original 3-Bay Station

Left to right: Mark, Colleen, Larry

Paul & Betty

Paul & Betty

Paul Zurcher at age 85